# The Rediscovery
## of the Holy Land
## in the Nineteenth Century

YEHOSHUA BEN-ARIEH

*There are many ways of writing a geography ...*
*some are wearisome and some vain ...*
*What is needed ... is to give a vision of*
*the Land as a whole ... and help you to hear*
*through it the sound of running history.*

(From George Adam Smith's, *The Historical Geography*
*of the Holy Land*, London 1894)

# The Rediscovery
# of the Holy Land
# in the Nineteenth Century

YEHOSHUA BEN-ARIEH

JERUSALEM — DETROIT, 1979
THE MAGNES PRESS / THE HEBREW UNIVERSITY
ISRAEL EXPLORATION SOCIETY
WAYNE STATE UNIVERSITY PRESS

Published in the United States and Canada
by Wayne State University Press,
Detroit, Michigan 48202

Copyright © 1979
by The Magnes Press, The Hebrew University
and the Israel Exploration Society,
Jerusalem

The first Hebrew edition was published by
The Israel Exploration Society and
Carta Jerusalem
Library of Congress Catalog Card Number 79-67619
ISBN 0-8143-1654-9

Designed by Typograph
Printed in Israel
at Attali Press, Jerusalem
Bound by John Dekker and Sons,
Grand Rapids, Michigan, United States of America

# PREFACE

The aim of this essay is twofold: to tell the story of the exploration of the Holy Land in the 19th century, and to create the basis for a further study of the historical geography of Israel in modern times.

The geographical exploration of the Holy Land forms a fascinating chapter in the long history of the country. Until the beginning of the 19th century the Land of Israel was virtually a *terra incognita* from a scientific point of view. After having been a closed book for many generations, the land of the Bible was rediscovered by the civilized world and, by the end of the century, the foundations for the scientific study of the country were firmly laid down.

Early in the course of my research in the historical geography of Israel, it became obvious that what happened here in the 19th century held the key to understanding the geographical developments of our own times. It is commonly accepted that the modern era in the Middle East began at the turn of the 18th century with Napoleon's invasion of Egypt and Palestine. The following 80 years, or so, witnessed significant changes in the character and appearance of the ancient Land of Israel. During this time, much was written about the country, making it possible for us to reconstruct the physical and social landscape of those days before it was "spoilt" by modern development. Most of the writers were travellers who visited Palestine and the surrounding regions in ever-increasing numbers as the century progressed. While working through this seemingly inexhaustible material, I realized that it would be necessary, first of all, to assess the nature of this literature by gauging the reliability of its authors. This book, therefore, deals mainly with the sources of information for the period, and evaluates these from a geographical and historical point of view.

The following account of the rediscovery of Palestine in the 19th century, is divided into five sections, reflecting contemporary political developments. The last chapter is an exception in that it centers on the activities of the Palestine Exploration Fund rather than on any focal political event. Each of the five chapters begins with a brief historical review of the various changes — political, administrative, and demographic — that

5

occurred in Palestine and the surrounding areas during the period under review. The subsections, which discuss particular topics within the general framework of the discovery of the country, also follow a chronological order.

The many illustrations form an important part of this work. They are reproductions of original drawings, sketches, engravings, and etchings that graced much of this literature. Only contemporary works have been included in order to preserve the spirit of the period.

The spelling of the place-names generally follows that of the official maps of the Israel Department of Surveys. A few exceptions reflect traditionally accepted spellings, such as Safed, Jaffa, etc. In some cases, where this can help in identifying a site, the Arabic place-name is added in parentheses.

The names of all the authors mentioned in the bibliographical list of primary sources are printed in bold characters the first time they appear in the text.

The groundwork for this essay was begun in 1965-6 when I spent a sabbatical year at the Department of Geography of University College, London, at that time under Professor H.C. Darby. A Hebrew edition was brought out in 1970 by Carta Jerusalem in cooperation with the Israel Exploration Society. Subsequently, I published several articles on some of the more important explorers of the Holy Land that are discussed in these pages, and wrote a book, *A City Reflected in its Times, Jerusalem in the Nineteenth Century. The Old City* (as yet only in Hebrew). The present work represents a revision and expansion of the Hebrew version and incorporates the results of additional research and study, especially material gathered for my book on Jerusalem.

The maps and illustrations accompanying the text are identical to those in the Hebrew edition. Some of these were taken from the archives of the Palestine Exploration Fund; others were prepared at the photographic laboratory of University College, London; many were reproduced directly from books at the Jewish National and University Library, the Library of the Israel Department of Antiquities at Rockefeller Museum, and the Yad Ben Zvi Institute Library, all three in Jerusalem. My thanks go to them all.

The book has profited from the assistance of my colleagues at the Geography Department and other departments of the Hebrew University. I am also indebted to the many readers of the Hebrew edition who provided me with their response and remarks.

To Joseph Shadur, the editor of this book, who helped me much, not only with translations and arrangement of the material, but also with advice and remarks; to Ruth Perlman, who prepared the index; to Attali Printing Services for their fine printing; to the Israel Exploration Society and its Director, Yosef Aviram; and to the Magnes Press and its Director, Ben-Zion Yehoshua, who saw the book through to its present, attractive format, my gratitude is due as well.

The Hebrew University                                          Y. BEN-ARIEH
Jerusalem, March 1979

# TABLE OF CONTENTS

# INTRODUCTION

At the beginning of the 19th century Palestine was but a derelict province of the decaying Ottoman Empire. The Sublime Porte only showed interest in it because of the holy places and the meagre revenue extorted from the wretched inhabitants. The country was badly governed, having no political importance of its own; its economy was primitive; the sparse, ethnically mixed population subsisted on a dismally low standard; the few towns were small and miserable; the roads few and neglected. In short, Palestine was but a sad backwater of a crumbling empire — a far cry from the fertile, thriving land it had been in ancient times.

In the course of the century the country was slowly brought into the orbit of European interests and subjected to modern influences. Napoleon Bonaparte focussed the attention of the civilized world on this remote corner of the Mediterranean by invading it in 1799. In 1831 Mohammed Ali, of Egypt, quarreling with his Ottoman overlords, occupied Palestine and Syria and ruled these provinces for nine years.

Fearing the total collapse of the Ottoman Empire, the European powers intervened to restore the Sultan's authority and drove the Egyptians out. But such help had its price: the system of capitulations was extended, and foreign consulates were set up one after another throughout the Empire. The religious awakening resulting from renewed interest in the Holy Land took acute form in clashes between the various Christian churches. Lurking behind these conflicts were the European states contesting control of the holy places — in particular of the Church of the Holy Sepulchre. The religious dispute even served as one of the pretexts for the Crimean War, following which, the powers substantially extended their influence and deepened their intervention in the Ottoman Empire. In the late fifties work began on the Suez Canal, and thirteen years after its completion in 1869, the British occupied Egypt and cast their eyes on the patch of land imperial conquerors always regarded as an invaluable strategic base.

From the 1840's, changes began to take place in the physical appearance of Palestine. The towns in particular took on a new aspect: post offices were set up, transport services were extended, ties with the world strengthened, and open spaces filled in with new buildings. However, these

11

were only the mere buds of growth. Really significant change in the country's topography occurred in the seventies and eighties with the establishment of the first modern agricultural settlements by the German Templegesellschaft, the marked increase in Jewish population, and the Zionist movement.

It is not the purpose of this survey to go into the historical and political events or to deal with the economic developments that took place during the last two decades of the century, but rather to concentrate on one subject — the exploration of the Holy Land and its rediscovery during the 19th century.

At the beginning of the 19th century, Palestine was a virtual *terra incognita* from a scientific point of view. Europeans had not ventured into many of its regions for many generations. Very few explorers had studied the natural history or the flora and fauna of the land; what maps existed were merely crude sketches lacking precision and detail. The extent to which European civilization was ignorant of the physical geography of the country is illustrated by the fact that, until 1835, experts had determined the latitudes of only ten inhabited areas, and in the 1820's topographical altitude was measured for the first time according to the boiling point of water! Until the mid-thirties, no one had noticed that the Jordan depression is several hundred metres lower than the Mediterranean, and it was only ten years later that the correct level of the Dead Sea was determined.

In the course of the 19th century, the country began to unveil its secrets. It fascinated the explorers. At first they followed the main thoroughfares, then they moved on to secondary roads, and finally ventured along hidden and unknown paths, registering observation points and conducting surveys. Geographical and historical research were the culmination of this interest.

Exploring the Holy Land was unlike the penetration of Africa or the discovery of other unknown regions. Here, even the unknown was somehow familiar. The Bible, Josephus, the writings of the church fathers, Crusader chronicles — all seemed to come alive out of the dusty ruins and the forsaken landscape. To this day, archaeological discoveries in Israel have this familiar quality about them. The same spirit permeated even the study of the physical characteristics and the natural history of Palestine.

It soon became plain that very little was known of the country, and travellers now gripped by a desire to discover and learn, set out to locate settlement sites, identify historical places, and determine geographical points

12

according to astronomical observations and measurements. They chose their routes with great care, proceeded with compass in hand, listed and described details along their way, measured distances by the time they could be covered on horseback, and tried to sketch all they saw.

Wayfarers, travellers, research expeditions and scientific groups dedicated themselves to revealing the country's natural and human landscape. In the latter part of the 19th century, the Palestine Exploration Fund carried out mapping and survey projects that fundamentally clarified the topographical structure of the country and resulted in the first exact, large-scale map. They described towns, villages, and the people, and laid the foundations for the study of geology, climatic conditions, plant and animal life, and for the history of settlement in various periods — but mainly in the time of the Bible. Henceforth, every attempt at further study of the land was bound to refer to the monumental work of the Palestine Exploration Fund. Although much new knowledge constantly comes to light and research and exploration continue even today, the foundations of modern scientific investigation of the country were firmly laid down by the 1880's.

The first eighty years of the 19th century, then, were the great era of the geographical exploration of Palestine. Its heroes, the Western travellers and explorers and their work and writings, form the subject of our story.

Palestine antedated other Eastern countries as the focus of European attention and interest. Since the Babylonian exile, Jews had prayed and yearned for a return to their ancient homeland, while Christians revered it as the Holy Land. The motives behind pilgrimages and visits were mainly religious — to follow in the footsteps of Jesus, to see the holy places, and to pray there.

In previous centuries few Western travellers had ventured on the long and arduous journey, their numbers fluctuating with political conditions and the upsurge of religious passion. Until the beginning of the 19th century many of them had recorded their journeys, concerning themselves mainly with the holy sites and their adventures in reaching these. Some of these writings contained advice to future travellers who might follow in their footsteps. In the first third of the 19th century, the stream of European travellers began to swell, and interest in Palestine underwent a marked change. The compulsion to explore and understand the geography of the country was added to the thrill of discovery. Travellers no longer confined themselves to the holy places. The sum-total of information on the

13

country became increasingly richer and more accurate than what could be gleaned from the writings of pilgrims of earlier centuries, although it took some time before acceptable scientific standards were reached.

Works written in the first half of the 19th century still show many shortcomings: most of the travellers kept to safe roads, and, since they did not get to see all parts of the country, their accounts were limited in scope; their reliance on information supplied by local guides and Arab villagers led to the incorporation of hearsay and fanciful traditions. Moreover they were greatly influenced by the accounts of earlier authors and by the use of antiquated maps, many details in their books being simply copied from these. Consequently, maps of the period were usually drawn to small scale and lacked many features and precision — reflecting the meagre geographical knowledge of the map-makers. These maps mainly attempted to indicate historical sites but even for this the existing knowledge was scant.

We can assess the writings of these early 19th century travellers from several points of view. On the one hand, they are quaint and often amusing when read with the wisdom of hindsight. But on the other hand, interspersed among the repetitive accounts of their itineraries are many incidental remarks and observations that provide us with details of the landscapes traversed and the people met on the way. Even if they did not set out to explore the country but to visit holy places and historical sites, they unwittingly contributed new information on the state of the country and its people. These "by-products", are of great value for the reconstruction of the historical geography of Palestine in the 19th century. They enable us to trace the settlement patterns of the period and to understand the life-styles, occupations, social organisation, etc. of the inhabitants.

As might be expected, the quality and standard of writing of these travel books vary greatly. Few of the traveller-authors were perceptive or reliable, or had sufficient background knowledge to judge intelligently what was worth recording. Most dwelt on their personal discomforts and petty concerns.

Their importance to us depends upon the subjects we are interested in. For instance, some of these books provide interesting insights for the study of the Jews of Palestine, for the authors often dealt with this subject. On the other hand, this literature is virtually useless to the archaeologist, either because it contains nothing about the country's antiquities, or because the writers lacked the capacity and knowledge for understanding the importance of what they observed. Our yardstick in evaluating these works will be the extent of their contribution to the furtherance of knowledge about Palestine in general, and the material they provide for reconstructing the human landscape at the time of their visits.

The 19th century saw many travellers making their way to Palestine, and a plethora of books were produced in many languages. But the large number, in contrast with the paucity of useful information they provide, raises difficulties in the selective perusal of this literature. Sometimes the authenticity of one important detail is the only compensation in thousands of lines of verbiage. The famous German geographer, Carl Ritter, who toiled his way through much of this literature remarked that "In order to obtain even single grains of gold it has often been necessary... to pull to pieces great heaps of rubbish."

Much of these writings sprang from the urge to confirm Biblical passages, whether these referred to the past or to prophecy. Some authors advanced original ideas to prove their theories. Others were dragged into theological disputes in attempts at justifying their findings.

Reinhold **Röhricht** in his *Bibliotheca Geographica Palaestinae* points out that between 1800 and 1878, about two thousand traveller-authors produced at least one book, publication, or article each. But, in fact, most authors produced more than one book or article, making a total of at least five thousand published items on Palestine in that span of time. It is not our aim here to present a full catalogue of these travel books, or to compose a compendium of the results of Palestine exploration, but rather to deal with the landmarks in the development of knowledge about Palestine. We will try to single out those of the traveller-authors whose writings contain important material for the reconstruction of the historical geography of Palestine throughout the 19th century.

Most of the travelogues are enlivened by illustrations — reproductions of paintings, sketches, and drawings. Many artists came to the country to portray its places of interest and scenery. Consequently, among the travel books are a number in which pictures form the primary content, the text serving merely to explain these.

Already in previous centuries, some travellers came mainly to depict the holy places. But since the Muslim authorities frowned upon such departures from usual pilgrim behaviour, many of these drawings were made furtively and were often inaccurate. Back home, the views were cut on wood blocks or engraved on copper plates to be reprinted many times

15

over the centuries as illustrations of such travel books. The artists of the 19th century, like the authors of travel books, differed from their predecessors in approach to their subject matter. Their drawings were more realistic; and, besides the principal holy places, they portrayed landscapes and facets of the life of the population. These illustrations are significant from a historical-geographical point of view, and, because of their precision and detail, it is often possible to locate the artist's exact observation point. Yet, these pictures were, of course, made by hand and shaped by the talent and inspiration of the artist. Often there were considerable discrepancies between them and reality. To prepare these views for printing, they had to be traced or redrawn mirror-wise on wood blocks or metal plates, and engraved by men who had never seen the original sites. The compositions were usually altered somewhat, in keeping with the style of the period, and the results were sometimes at variance with the originals.

In the first half of the century the artist's task was not yet free of danger in the remoter parts. Sometimes sketching involved a risk to life owing to the hostility of the Muslim inhabitants, who regarded the work as an act of defilement — a desecration of the holy places by representing them on paper. However, with the Egyptian conquest in 1831, security improved in Palestine and many artists made the difficult journey to the Holy Land to sketch scenes their predecessors had not dared to attempt. They marvelled at the country, but were appalled by its state of desolation.

What impelled these artists and talented amateurs to draw so many pictures? The scenes of the Holy Land certainly captured their imagination, but there also seemed to have been an insatiable market in the Western world for such views and illustrations. Consequently, during this period, many books on Palestine and on sacred subjects were decorated and illustrated with views of the country.

To what extent pictures of Palestine became fashionable can be judged by a practice common at the time among travellers. Besides describing their adventures, they would make on-the-spot sketches and bring them back to professional artists to be reworked as paintings. Moreover, the artists yearning to see for themselves the scenes they were asked to compose from the sketches of others, came to the country and redid their work with a greater measure of accuracy and success.

Travel drawings were fashionable not only of Palestine. Many of the visiting artists in the 19th century produced similar illustrations also of the neighbouring countries, Egypt, Transjordan, and Syria, and, of course, of other parts of the world as well.

The artists did not only depict the people and landscapes but also set out to record geographical phenomena and recent discoveries in Palestine and the surrounding regions. A favourite subject was the Jordan depression and the Dead Sea — the lowest point on earth. Similarly, they recorded unusual architectural elements, springs, indigenous trees and plants, as well as coins and ancient remains found throughout the country.

At the beginning of the 1850's the scenery of Palestine came into the focus of the camera — the recorder of unadorned, naked truth. It was no longer necessary to rely solely on sketches and drawings seen subjectively, and often emotionally; we now find nature represented as it is, with all the details overlooked by the eye of the artist. However, photographs did not immediately answer the needs of publishers for only after several decades did it become technically possible to prepare printing blocks for pictures directly from photographs. Until then photographs were pasted separately in each copy of the book. Consequently, the photographs were usually handed over to an artist, who reproduced them in the form of an engraving — a technique then at the height of its popularity. The utilization of photographs for wood, copper, and steel engravings brought a greater degree of precision into the portrayals of landscape.

Our story begins one year before the dawn of the 19th century — Bonaparte's invasion of Palestine in 1799 marked the beginning of modern times in the country as well as in the entire Middle East.

*Bridge over the Brook Kidron. (Luigi Mayer, 1804).*

A few years after the French invasion, a collection appeared of ten rather fanciful coloured prints after drawings by Luigi Mayer. The accompanying text, by Ernst Rosenmüller, describes each picture and provides a brief introduction to Palestine — its geographic position and history, and the condition of its agriculture. The imposing mortuary monuments in the Kidron valley stirred the imagination of most travellers and became a favourite subject of artists. The little arched bridge over the Kidron, opposite "Absalom's Tomb", has since disappeared.

# CHAPTER ONE

# THE FIRST THIRTY YEARS (1799-1831)
# TRAVELLERS IN DISGUISE

*Pool of Birket Isra'il, Jerusalem. (Luigi Mayer, 1804).*

Birket Isra'il, at that time identified with the Pool of Bethesda, was a site of special attraction to 19th century travellers. This large pool was adjacent to the outside wall of the Haram enclosure at its north-eastern corner, inside the Old City wall near the Lions Gate. The first visitors of this period found the pool dry, but sewage from the adjacent houses enabled wild plants and fruit trees to flourish in it. In other drawings of the period, the pool does not appear as well-preserved and, in the 1930's, it was filled in with earth and levelled off.

# BEGINNINGS OF THE MODERN PERIOD
# NAPOLEON INVADES PALESTINE
# THE GEOGRAPHICAL CONTRIBUTION

In January 1799, French troops of Napoleon Bonaparte's army in Egypt crossed the Sinai desert by way of El Arish and swept north along the Mediterranean coast of Palestine in an attempt to reach Constantinople. It was the first time since the expulsion of the Crusaders from Akko (Acre) in 1291 that Palestine came under consideration by the Western powers for anything but its holy places. Napoleon's bold move was not only a challenge to Ottoman sovereignty: it was an open attempt at severing Britain's lines of communication with India. Combined operations by the pasha of Akko, Ahamed Jazzar, representing the Ottoman sultan, and the English fleet under Sir Sidney Smith, stopped Napoleon's advance at Akko and forced the retreat of the French to Egypt.

On its way back, in June 1799, the French army left destruction, plague, and death in its wake. Eye-witnesses described the coastal strip, from the Carmel to Gaza, as one huge blaze of fire. Napoleon's soldiers destroyed all fortifications, laid waste the villages, and burned the crops.

But the French invasion of Palestine made an important contribution to the science of Palestine geography. Accompanying Napoleon's forces in Egypt was a corps of French geographers and engineers whose surveys were later brought out in atlas form, known as *Jacotin's Map* after its chief editor, an officer in the corps. The map contains 47 folios, covering the main regions of Egypt — especially Lower Egypt — and six folios, to a scale of 1:100,000, of parts of Palestine: El Arish, Gaza, Jerusalem, Caesarea, Akko–Nazareth–the Jordan, and Tyre and Sidon. Surveying for the maps was, of course, limited to areas under French control. A triangulation grid was laid down with its base in the Akko plain. Grid determination and partial measurements were carried out largely with a compass and the distances measured-off in paces, initially to Ras el Abiad (the White Cape), then to Mount Carmel, and finally to the east side of the Jezreel Valley, until Lower Galilee was demarcated. This area, therefore, was measured more carefully than others in the country. The other

21

regions, mainly the mountains of Samaria, were only hurriedly surveyed from horseback. Mapping reached as far inland as Jerusalem, Nablus, Lake Kinneret (the Sea of Galilee), the Hula Valley, and up to the Litani River in the north. Because of the absence of astronomical points and ignorance of the latitudes, the coastline from Gaza to Akko was determined as being one degree east of its actual position. This error led to many others which were only rectified in the 1840's.

Besides those parts of the maps drawn up according to measurements, there were regions for which the only data given was based on hearsay. For want of anything better, the French cartographers relied on information provided by Arab guides about areas they had never themselves visited. Consequently, such regions appear inaccurately in the map. Errors were caused in part by the absence of astronomical data, a factor which led the map-makers to indicate place-names according to details gleaned from the reports and observations of earlier travellers. Moreover, large areas of the maps, such as the eastern part of Samaria and the coastal strip between Ashqelon and Gaza, were left altogether blank.

Sometimes the map makers, not wishing to publish a map with empty spaces, filled-in areas with symbols of plants and sites. Thus the area west of Jerusalem was covered with stylized trees and bushes, while geographical data was altogether absent.

Despite all this, Jacotin's map is a very valuable historical document of conditions in Palestine at the turn of the 18th century. The notion of mountains, rivers, settlements, historical sites, roads, khans, and, in part, the type of agriculture, etc., is a worthwhile contribution to geographical science. The maps were printed in French and Arabic, but most of the names — except for those of major places — are confused, either having been inadequately checked, or as a result of insufficient knowledge of the language of the country. Many villages are marked simply "village" of no particular name; the names of some of the rivers are not the same as in later maps and the descriptions of plants and crops are inexact. It is difficult to believe that the cultivated areas were marked on the map as a result of field surveys; they are only noted as a vague indication of their location.

Nevertheless, the maps afford valuable information on the cultural landscape of the country. Many military and historical details appear: Napoleon's campaign routes, the line of advance or retreat of every unit,

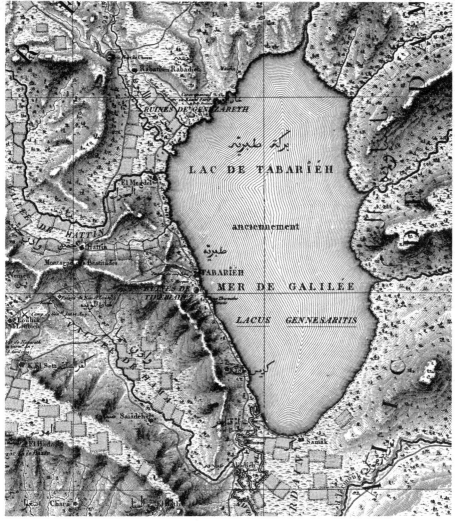

*Section of Jacotin's map showing the Sea of Galilee — 1799. (Jacotin, 1810).*

Jacotin's map, published in 1810, was hurriedly prepared when Napoleon invaded Palestine and is thus inferior to contemporary European topographical maps. Although it is more comprehensive and accurate than previous maps of Palestine, it belongs essentially to the type of maps made by travellers on the spot from azimuth readings determined by compass. Jacotin's map, however, marks the beginning of the modern mapping of Palestine, for the French cartographers employed the most advanced methods of mathematics, astronomy, surveying, and printing known at the time.

23

names of commanders, battle sites and dates according to the calendar of the French Revolution, times of setting out and giving battle, and so on.

For forty years Jacotin's map served as the basis for the cartography of Palestine, and makes it possible for us today to trace the stages in the transformation of the country's landscape in the 19th century. It is particularly enlightening when compared with the descriptions of travellers and the maps of the Palestine Exploration Fund published 80 years later.

Among the sources describing the French campaigns in Palestine from an English point of view, and giving information on the state of the country, are the letters of the British admiral, Sir Sydney Smith, whose fleet helped Ahmed Jazzar in the war against Napoleon. These, together with Bonaparte's letters, were appended to General **Bertrand**'s narrative of the campaign in Egypt and Palestine. Interesting observations on the plague and other diseases rampant in the Ottoman Empire were dealt with in the book by the surgeon, William **Wittman**, who accompanied the Turkish army and the British fleet in the years 1799-1801.

Shortly after the defeat of the French a renowned traveller, Edward **Clarke**, who undertook many expeditions in European and Asian countries, published a series of heavy volumes on his travels. He only spent seventeen days in Palestine, some of them in Akko, where he arrived on 29 June 1801. From here he went via Nazareth to Tiberias and Lake Kinneret, past Lavi (Lubiya) and Mt. Tabor to Nablus, Jerusalem, Bethlehem, and Jaffa, and finally returned to Akko. He tells of his meetings with Jazzar Pasha and describes the life of the latter's subjects in Akko.

Clarke is typical of many North-European Protestants who doubted the genuineness of the traditionally accepted sites as pointed out by local Christians and the Franciscan monks. They often tried to discover "rival" holy places, going to great lengths to justify their identifications. Although he was not thoroughly acquainted with the country, Clarke had his own theories about some of the sites he visited. His descriptions of these places are extremely beautiful, but his conclusions are generally unfounded.

We have an interesting collection of views from the hand of J.B. **Spilsbury**, a doctor on the British ship *Tiger* that came to the assistance of besieged Akko in 1799. After the French retreat to Egypt, he rambled through the

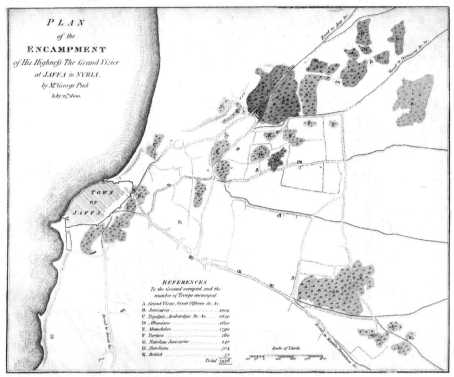

*Jaffa and its environs — 1800. (Wittman, 1803, p. 226).*

Accompanying the British and Turkish troops in pursuit of the French army, Wittman saw the destruction caused by Napoleon's retreating soldiers. His book also provides interesting details about the natural landscape and the cultivated parts of Palestine. It has numerous coloured prints of drawings and sketches, among which this sketch map of Jaffa and its vicinity. Other artists, too, depicted this area; the extensive groves and plantations around the town impressed many travellers at the beginning of the century.

25

country and captured its landscape with his pencil, depicting scenes of the native people and their way of life. Spilsbury's drawings were reproduced and published in book form in 1803. One of Spilsbury's pictures portrays the Ottoman governor of Akko, Ahmed Jazzar, who ruled his subjects with an iron hand. Other drawings show natural vistas, buildings in Akko, mosques and the market-place, inhabitants in festive dress, the ruins of Caesarea and Atlit seen from the sea, the French army camp in the Jezreel Valley at the foot of Mt. Tabor, Khan Jubb Yusif, the Benot Ya'aqov Bridge (Bridge of Jacob's Daughters) over the Jordan, etc.

William **Cooper**, a chaplain on one of the ships of the English fleet, also took the opportunity to travel in the Holy Land. After the fighting ended, he left the ship at Akko to tour and draw the country and its surroundings. His book, published in London in 1822, contains a collection of sketches accompanying geographical and historical texts in English and French. Thanks to the Rev. Cooper we have an idea of Haifa in those days — a small settlement on the shore of the bay, surrounded by a wall, with a small citadel above it. Cooper did not omit to immortalize himself in this picture, showing himself engrossed in his work.

# THE PASHAS — UPHOLDERS OF TURKISH RULE

The failure of Napoleon's campaign brought about the return of Turkish rule to all parts of the country in the person of Ahmed Jazzar, "the Butcher". The man who successfully resisted the conqueror of Egypt was as renowned among the Arabs as he was in Europe.

Although Jazzar Pasha's career was unusual in several ways, it also reflects the relationship between the pashas of Palestine and the local population on the one hand, and between the pashas and the Sublime Porte on the other.

Despite his powerful position, Jazzar chose to remain loyal to the Porte, and, on the whole, paid the revenues due to the sultan in Constantinople. But within his own area he acted as an independent ruler. He built up a private army and fleet, levied taxes and custom duties at will, and even sought to maintain a monopoly on certain branches of local and foreign trade. Occasionally, he himself administered justice, passing sentences and having them carried out on the spot, including mutilation and the death penalty. His rule was typical of that of other pashas at a time when Ottoman imperial structure was weakening. The provincial governors knew well how to exploit the weaknesses of the central government by illegally assuming extensive prerogatives. By the end of the 18th century, the pashas of Palestine and Syria had become virtually independent, maintaining their power as long as they could thwart measures taken by the imperial government against them.

Jazzar Pasha died after a thirty-year reign of terror on 7 May 1804. Right to the end he kept up his ruthless ways, and, long after the French had gone, he engaged in plundering campaigns throughout the country. Safed, Nazareth, and Ramallah, among other places, were mercilessly pillaged. At one point, the "Butcher" threatened to massacre the native Christians, claiming that they had assisted Napoleon. Only the intervention of the British admiral, Sir Sydney Smith, prevented this tragedy. Smith stayed in the area several years. In 1801, he marched his sailors from the coast to Jerusalem and Bethlehem, with drums beating and flags flying, in demonstration of Christian power.

Rivalry and warfare broke out among the claimants to the pasha's seat when Jazzar died. Finally Suleiman Pasha managed to consolidate his authority and "governed" for fourteen years, from 1804 to 1818.

Under his rule, the country sank deeper into poverty and wild Bedouin tribesmen wandered through it unchecked. However, compared with the Jazzar regime, it was a time of peace and relative prosperity. The local ruler of the central coastal plain of Palestine, Mohammed Abu Nabut, rebuilt Jaffa, adding walls and fortifications. Shortly before his death, Suleiman expelled Abu Nabut who found a haven in Egypt with Mohammed Ali. The central coastal strip — Emeq Hefer, the Sharon, and the Jaffa district — passed under the direct control of the governor of Akko in 1819.

Suleiman was succeeded by his beloved slave Abdallah Ibn Ali. After initial skirmishes with the governor of Damascus, and by bribing himself out of military defeat, Abdallah Pasha continued to rule with a strong hand and legendary cruelty until the Egyptian conquest of 1831.

In the years 1800-1831, Palestine was divided administratively into two Ottoman provinces (pashaliks), their borders varying with the military

27

*St. Jean d'Acre with Mount Carmel in the distance. (Carne, 1836, I, p. 29).*

Ahmed Jazzar, the despotic and cruel ruler of Acre from 1775 to 1804, tried to win over his subjects and, at the same time, give visible proof of his power. He beautified his capital by repairing the city wall, renovating the khans, constructing markets, restoring the aqueduct from the Kabri springs and, above all, by building the large mosque that still bears his name. Ancient Acre, unlike Jaffa, was built on a plain, and from outside, most of its buildings were hidden by the city walls. To stress the importance of the mosque in the life of the city, Jazzar built it to tower above the walls, giving it a splendid effect from afar. The many-arched bazaar to the left of the mosque courtyard was also new; the remains in the foreground were part of the fortress destroyed by Ibrahim Pasha. The drawn-in outline of the Carmel range in the background is fairly exact; Haifa, at the foot of the mountain, appears as a white blob on the far side of the bay.

28

*Fords of the Jordan. (Horne, 1836. p. 17).*

"One of the fords of the Jordan, pretty nearly at the same ford over which the Israelites passed on their first entering the promised land, found the stream extremely rapid.
Its depth here is stated to be not more than four feet. This ford is delineated in our
engraving; and in the foreground are pilgrims collected for the purposes of bathing in
its hallowed waters. The annual procession for this purpose takes place after the festival of Easter. The pilgrims quit the Holy City under the protection of the governor of
Jerusalem and his guards who defend them from the assaults of the plundering Arabs
of the district ... After riding along the bank for about two miles ... the pilgrims reach
the spot delineated in our view; they then immediately strip, and rushing down the
steep bank, plunge into the sacred stream. Many carry with them a white robe, to
wear at the ceremony. When they are clothed again, and have filled their bottles with
the holy water, they return to Jerusalem."

29

strength of their governors. Generally though, the areas consisted of the mountain area, from a point north of Nablus to south of Hebron — including Jerusalem — belonging to the pashalik of Damascus, and of Galilee and the coastal plain which were part of the pashalik of Sidon.

Most of Transjordan, the Negev, and Sinai during this period were outside the effective control of the Ottoman Empire. Within the pashaliks, the pashas regarded the collection of taxes as their main function. Rather than ensuring peace and security, the army served to terrorize the population for the purpose of tax collection. Under such conditions of general instability, the Bedouin moved freely through the populated areas and plundered the villages.

The fellaheen had their own internal self-defence organization based on a tribal group pattern dating to the Arab conquest of Syria and Palestine. The native Muslim Arabic-speaking population ranged themselves into two groups the "Qays" (northerners) and the "Yaman" (southerners) which long before had lost any original ethnic or geographical meaning.

Blood feuds among the fellaheen of 19th century Palestine often took the form of open warfare between "Qays" and "Yaman" factions, the pashas seldom attempting to enforce the peace undermined by these conflicts and, on the contrary, exploiting them to their own advantage.

Economic developments in the Ottoman Empire greatly influenced the government of Palestine. At the beginning of the 19th century, the empire reached a new political nadir when nationalist rebellions broke out in its European provinces. In 1815 the Greek islands freed themselves from Ottoman suzerainty, and England extended them her protection. In 1821, the mainland Greeks revolted and even Abdallah, the governor of Akko, was ordered to assist the central government in quelling the insurrection.

In 1826 Abdallah sent help to Beirut which was being bombarded by a Greek flotilla. On the outbreak of the Greek revolt the Ottoman authorities in Palestine adopted a stricter policy towards the local Christian Greek Orthodox population. Abdallah was particularly severe with the Christians of Jaffa, Lod, and Ramla who were within his jurisdiction, earning him the epithet "Enemy of Christians."

Extortions of money from the population provoked local rebellions: in 1825 there was an uprising in Jerusalem and its surroundings when Mustafa Pasha, governor of Damascus, demanded full payment of the high tax quota. The troubles assumed such proportions that Sultan Mahmoud II had to order the governor of Akko to occupy Jerusalem and return it to the wali of Damascus.

After bombarding it for two weeks, Abdallah took the city at the end of 1826. The wali of Damascus was then ordered to garrison it. But the country was not pacified. In the mountains of Nablus a fellaheen revolt led by the local sheikhs broke out and spread south to Hebron and north to Safed.

The rule of Abdallah was thus beset with incessant rebellion and uprising. Quelled in one place, new clashes broke out elsewhere. Sometimes the rebellions were instigated by the local sheikhs to settle inter-tribal or inter-clan scores in quarrels that had nothing to do with the authorities. Nevertheless, despite its disturbed state, Palestine on the eve of the Egyptian conquest was under one single authority.

During these first turbulent thirty years of the 19th century, several explorers reached the country and managed to lay the first foundations for the scientific exploration of Palestine. Among them, two outstanding personalities, **Seetzen** and **Burckhardt**, well deserve the title of pioneers of Palestine research.

# PIONEERS OF RESEARCH: SEETZEN AND BURCKHARDT

Ulrich Jasper Seetzen, born in Northern Germany, displayed an early interest in the natural sciences and a love for travel. He studied medicine, and in his free time toured the European continent. On 13 June 1802, having decided to extend his travels to include the lands of the East and Africa, Seetzen set out for Constantinople.

Before his departure he studied and read about the places he was to visit, equipping himself with maps and directives from scientists of his acquaintance. Furthermore, he undertook to send antiquities and archaeological finds back to the Gotha Museum in Germany, and to note and copy inscriptions in Latin, Greek, Arabic, and Hebrew. Fully aware of the dangers inherent in such an expedition, he studied Arabic and Oriental customs, dressed in Arab garb, and outwardly adopted the religion of Islam. His experiences on the journey were recorded in a carefully kept diary.

At the beginning of his travels Seetzen had little or no money, but his successes as an antique collector soon brought him fame. Not only the Duke of Saxe-Gotha and the local museum, but later the Czar of Russia and other wealthy princes contributed to finance his trips.

Seetzen spent some time in Turkey, further familiarizing himself with the Oriental way of life. On 23 November, he arrived in Aleppo, remaining there over a year to complete his studies of Arabic. He acquired a number of antiquities and manuscripts which he dispatched to the museum, together with information and observations concerning the geography of Arab lands and a report on the Wahabi tribes in the Persian Gulf area.

In May 1805, Seetzen reached Damascus from where he set out on his tours of the Horan, Lebanon, Western Palestine, Transjordan, and Sinai. In Upper Galilee he visited Banias (Ceasarea Philippi), which had not been described by any European traveller since Crusader times. After exploring the Golan, he travelled through the district of Belkah-Gilead (May 1806), and discovered the magnificent remains of Gerasa (Jerash) and Philadelphia (Amman).

Seetzen then crossed the Jordan River and went to Jerusalem. In April and November 1806, he carried out tours in the vicinity of Jerusalem (Mount of Olives and the Tombs of the Kings), Bethlehem, and Hebron. It was during these tours that he heard, for the first time, of a number of interesting sites along the route to Sinai. Before setting out to inspect these, however, Seetzen managed to visit much of the western, northern, and eastern parts of the Holy Land. From Jerusalem he went to Ramla, thence to the ancient port of Jaffa where he boarded a vessel which carried him northward to Akko and Tyre, with stops at Caesarea, Dor (Tantura), and Haifa. In his travels, Seetzen also visited Shefar'am, Rama, Nazareth, Kafr Kanna, Bet She'an, and Nablus. In December 1806, he went from Jerusalem to Jericho, touring the region west of the Dead Sea. During the months of January, February, and March 1807, he became the first explorer to journey around the Dead Sea. This expedition included a visit to the town of Kerak, east of the lake.

In March-April 1807, he departed from Jerusalem, and by way of Hebron, the Negev, and Sinai, reached the St. Catherine Monastery at the foot of the traditional Mount Sinai.

In May 1807, Seetzen reached the port of Suez, and on the 18th of that month, turned up in Cairo. Here he remained for nearly two years, till March 1809. In the guise of an Arab merchant named Musa el-Hakim ("the Physician"), he undertook trips to the Fayum and the pyramids. While in Cairo, Seetzen added several African tongues to his knowledge, receiving lessons from a slave-trader, to prepare himself for the continuation of his expedition.

From Cairo, Seetzen journeyed to Heliopolis. On the way he was grievously afflicted by the elements of nature. He mentions that he was nearly blinded by a series of violent sandstorms and the merciless sun. Undaunted, he boarded a ship bound for Jedda, in Arabia, and on 8 October 1809, arrived in Mecca as a pilgrim. Though it was forbidden, on pain of death, to sketch the Holy Qaaba, the sacred black stone, Seetzen did so. Passing on to Medina, he sketched the city plan, taking careful note of its various mosques. Then, travelling southward, he reached Yemen, visiting Hudeida, Sana, Taiz, and other cities. In his last letters, dated 14 and 17 November 1810, he described Arabian horses, the Hadramaut, and the South Arabian inscriptions he discovered there.

He next intended to travel down the coast of the Red Sea and eventually to enter Africa south of the equator, but his sudden death brought an end to his brave adventures.

The final fate of this courageous explorer is shrouded in mystery. In Mocha he loaded on camels the objects he had collected for Gotha, including his notes and sketches, and set out for Sana. Two days after he left he was found dead. It has been assumed that he was poisoned on the orders of the Imam of Sana and Taiz. Despite his Arab garb, he may have raised doubts in the minds of the local people as to his true identity. The fact that he carried specimens of snakes preserved in alcohol may have given him, in their eyes, the appearance of a witch-doctor. His ceaseless inspections and investigations, and his studies in astronomy also may have aroused mistrust and fear.

Unfortunately, Seetzen did not bequeath all his knowledge to the world. Much of it was never written down, although material gathered on his journeys was published in contemporary German and English scientific journals. It was only in the 1850's that his writings were collected in book form and published in Berlin in four volumes. The first three include Seetzen's diary and an introduction by Professor Kruse, the learned

*Portrait of James Silk Buckingham. (Buckingham, 1821. Frontispiece).*

Buckingham's works contain a large number of illustrations. But despite his claims for their originality, many were obviously copied and reworked from 18th, and even 17th, century engravings. Buckingham apologizes for including his own portrait in his book, explaining that he acceded to the artist's request; and when he saw the success with which the portrait was received, decided to make it the frontispiece of his book, being certain that his readers would be interested in seeing him as he looked during his travels in the East.

34

*Sheikh Ibrahim — Johann Lewis Burckhardt, in his Arab Bernouse.
(Burckhardt, 1821. Frontispiece).*

Seetzen and Burckhardt and other early 19th century explorers travelled in Arab dress. Burckhardt disguised himself from time to time as a gunpowder merchant, an emissary-priest of the Greek Patriarch in Damascus, and a doctor gathering medicinal herbs. A note in the margin of the picture states that the drawing was made in Cairo in 1817.

editor. These volumes appeared in 1854-5, while the fourth one, a commentary to Seetzen's travels, appeared later, in 1859.

The spheres of Seetzen's interest were varied and far-reaching. He devoted much time and attention to archaeology and antiquities, to mineralogy, botany, and zoology. Thus, for example, he copied hundreds of Greek inscriptions, collected rock and plant specimens, drew up a detailed table of different creeks and wadis in several regions, prepared reports on thoroughbred Arabian horses, and so forth.

Carl Ritter pointed out that Seetzen was less fortunate than his followers, for his writings are little known to scholars. This is still true today. However, Seetzen's diary represents a major contribution to the knowledge of the Holy Land.

The Swiss explorer, John Lewis (Johann Ludwig) Burckhardt did not intend following in the footsteps of his predecessor, Seetzen, nor to explore Palestine and the Levant. He yearned to discover and explore the unknown interior of Africa.

Burckhardt was born in Basel, but dissatisfied with the political situation in his country, abandoned it for London. There he became acquainted with the activities of the British Association for Promoting the Discovery of Interior Africa, and offered his services to the leaders of the Association, Sir Joseph Bankes and the Rev. Dr. Hamilton. In May 1808, a general meeting of the Association willingly accepted his offer.

The Association decided to send Burckhardt to explore the Niger region, a task in which several previous explorers had failed. In preparation for this dangerous mission it was decided that Burckhardt should be sent to Syria for two years to study Muslim languages and customs so that he could use an Arab disguise to facilitate his movements. As part of these preparations, he was asked to tour portions of Syria which had not yet been sufficiently explored by Europeans.

From an extract of a letter he sent to Bankes, dated Malta, 22 April 1809, we know that Burckhardt learned about Seetzen for the first time when he was on the way to Syria.

You will be much interested in hearing that at this moment an attempt is making to explore the Interior of Africa; and that I have unknowingly entered upon my expedition as rival to a gentleman who is probably by this time in the scene of action. I was allowed the perusal of a letter from Dr. Seetzen to Mr. Barker, who is a merchant of Malta, and brother to the British Consul at Aleppo. Dr. Seetzen is a German Physician, who was sent five or six years ago by the Duke of Saxe-Gotha into the Levant, to collect manuscripts and Eastern curiosities. He has resided for a considerable length of time at Constantinople, at Smyrna, at Aleppo, at Damascus, and for the last eighteen months at Cairo, from whence his letter to Mr. Barker is dated on the 9th of February last. After remarking that he had sent off from Cairo to Gotha a collection of fifteen hundred manuscripts and three thousand different objects of antiquity, he informs Mr. Barker that he is waiting for the next caravan to set out for Suez; that he means to go down the eastern coast of the Red Sea, and then entering Africa to the southward of the line, to explore its interior parts. Such are his expressions.

From Malta, Burckhardt sailed to Syria and reached Aleppo where he spent over a year studying the Arabic language and customs.

In the autumn of 1810, 22 September to 17 October, he made his first trip from Damascus to the Lebanon, passing through Banias (Caesarea Philippi) which Seetzen also visited. Burckhardt described the view from the ruins of Banias and dealt with the names of the various headwaters of the Jordan River. In November of the same year he made his first expedition to the unexplored region of the Horan.

In the winter of 1812 he journeyed from Aleppo to Damascus via the Orontes Valley, Tripoli, and Mount Lebanon, and in the spring he set out on a second journey to the Horan, this time reaching the springs of Hammat-Gader and the Golan region. In the Horan, Burckhardt was the first European to find inscriptions of the Hittite culture.

In June 1812, Burckhardt undertook yet another of his preparatory trips. His route took him from Damascus to Tiberias and Galilee. In Tiberias he unexpectedly met another European traveller, Michael Bruce, who suggested that he come with him to Nazareth to meet the famous Lady of the East, Hester Stanhope.

From Nazareth he continued with an Arab merchant's caravan through En-Dor, the brook at Tabor, and along the eastern side of the Jordan Valley as far as Kerak, east of the Dead Sea. In Kerak he started to search for the lost site of Petra. This ancient and long-forsaken city had, for many generations, lain hidden from the eyes of European travellers. Its rediscovery is perhaps the best known of Burckhardt's achievements.

To explain and justify his travels in the Mount Hor region near Wadi Musa, Burckhardt told the local Bedouin that he had made a solemn vow to

sacrifice a lamb in honour of Aaron, brother of Moses, who was buried —
according to tradition — on Mount Hor.

From Petra, Burckhardt continued across the Arava and the Sinai Desert
through Nakhl, to Suez and Cairo. Four years later in 1816, he returned
to Sinai and visited the St. Catherine Monastery in the southern part of
the peninsula, and the Gulf of Aqaba. From Cairo, Burckhardt made
many other trips to different parts of Egypt, went down the Nile to the
Sudan, crossed the mountains to the coast of the Red Sea, and also visited
several regions of Arabia. In the course of his investigations he joined a
convoy of pilgrims going to Mecca, leaving a detailed description of the
pilgrimage and of the religious ceremonies at Mecca itself.

Burckhardt was destined never to complete his main mission for he died
of dysentery in Cairo, in 1817, while preparing for his journey to the
Fezzan in Africa.

Of Burckhardt's writings, five books have been published. They include
valuable information on Egypt and Nubia, Syria, Palestine and Sinai,
Arabia, Arabic proverbs, and notes on the Bedouins. As an Oriental traveller Burckhardt is of very highest rank, being considered one of the most
brilliant and perceptive explorers of the Near East. Edward Robinson, the
Biblical scholar who laid the foundations of historical-geographical research of the Holy Land evaluated him thus:

Accurate, judicious, circumspect, persevering. He accomplished very much; yet all
this only was preparatory to the great object he had in view, viz., to penetrate into
the interior of Africa.

The achievement of Burckhardt in his explorations of Syria and the Holy
Land were summed up by the editor of his book as follows:

The principal geographical discoveries of our traveller are the nature of the country
between the Dead Sea and the Gulf of Aelana, now Akaba; the extent, conformation,
and detailed topography of the Hauran; the site of Apameia on the Orontes, one of
the most important cities of Syria under the Macedonian Greeks; the site of Petra,
which under the Romans gave the name of Arabia Petraea to the surrounding territory;
and the general structure of the peninsula of Mount Sinai; together with many new
facts of its geography.

It would be unfair to sum up Burckhardt's achievements in the exploration of the Holy Land without noting his efforts to reveal to Europe the
mysteries of the strange and unknown world of the Bedouin.

In the pages of his notes and writings, Burckhardt revealed himself as a man of sterling character. When, for example, he arrived at a place that had already been explored or described by a predecessor, he would never hesitate to give him due credit in his description; he was particularly careful in this regard concerning Seetzen. On the other hand, when the credit for a discovery was rightly his, Burckhardt's inherent modesty prevented him from drawing undue attention to the fact. Thus, he did not publicize his discovery of Petra — although Seetzen had in vain searched for this legendary desert city.

Notwithstanding his sufferings, Burckhardt never willingly faltered or deviated from his plans. He did give up a visit to Deraa and Basra in the Horan, but only because he could not find guides to accompany him on this dangerous journey. He tended to leave Greek inscriptions to the decision of the experts, apologized for not having completed his notes on a particular place or object because of the need to curtail his visits, and so on.

The personal achievements of Burckhardt and Seetzen regarding their travels, even in the limited territory of the Holy Land, may be summed up today as very substantial. Nevertheless, it is not only in these achievements that their importance rests. Their methods of work and the interest they stimulated in the country played a decisive role in the future exploration of the Holy Land.

Seetzen and Burckhardt did not know one another but there were many similarities in their methods of research. Neither went to seek out the holy places of Christianity, and they did not follow secure, well-travelled roads.

Their travels were mainly in the southern and eastern portions of the country, areas previous travellers had not visited and about which information was scanty. Burckhardt, for instance, did not even visit Jerusalem.

Thus, the ancient traditions did not influence their studies. This does not mean that they were not interested in the history of the country. On the contrary, before their visits both of them studied most of the literature written on the regions in which they travelled. They had their own criticism of these writings, especially the accounts of earlier travellers, but they tried to use every accurate fact that could be found in them.

The contribution of Seetzen and Burckhardt as pioneers in the scientific research into the history of the country was very important, but they

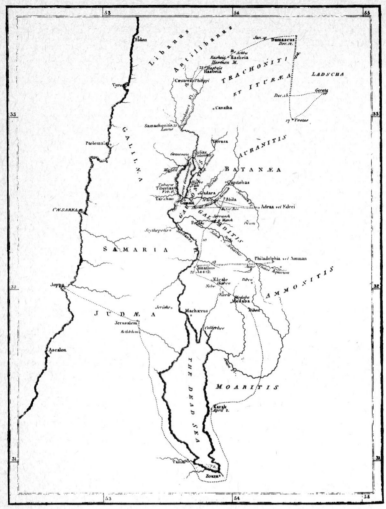

*Map of the Sea of Galilee and the Dead Sea — 1805-7. (Seetzen, 1810).*

Unfortunately Seetzen did not impart all his discoveries to the world, for much of them were never recorded. Although material gathered on his first journeys was initially published in contemporary German and English scientific journals, it was only in the fifties that his writings were collected in book form and published in Berlin. One of his entries, translated into English and published by the Palestine Association, was accompanied by a map of the area between Damascus and the Ghor (the lower Jordan Rift Valley). This map illustrates Seetzen's meagre cartographical knowledge. It is typical of the amateurish cartography of Palestine at the beginning of the nineteenth century.

40

also added to the cartographical and geographical knowledge of the land at the time. The map of the Sea of Galilee, the Jordan Valley, and the Dead Sea, published by the "Palestine Association" in London in 1810 together with Seetzen's report from the East, show the meagre cartographical knowledge of the country in those days. Nevertheless, Carl Ritter evaluates Seetzen's achievement as an important improvement, if not the beginning of the modern cartography of the Holy Land.

Burckhardt also contributed in this area. He took many field measurements and tried to delineate different physical characteristics of the country, but the results were not always accurate. The publishers of his book *Syria and the Holy Land* found it necessary to base the map accompanying his book mainly on other sources. They also felt the need to mention the defects and shortcomings of the tools and instruments at Burckhardt's disposal, the haste in which his expedition was carried out, the necessity of concealing his activities from his guides and fellow-travellers, and even his lack of experience in this kind of work. Despite all these, however, the fruits of his travels were of great importance in the detailed and profound descriptions of the Arava from which scholars began to develop the theory of the tectonic link between the Dead Sea and the Red Sea.

From the first, Seetzen and Burckhardt understood the significance of Arabic place names. Both compiled lists of names, chiefly from areas east of the Jordan. While examining these place names they concluded that the later Greek and Roman traditions of the foreign inhabitants of the Holy Land, had to be distinguished from the ancient Semitic ones preserved by the local population. They postulated that Greek names had disappeared from use while the ancient Hebrew names were imbedded in the roots of Arabic names.

Perhaps the most peculiar thing about their way of travelling was their need to assume Arab disguise and adopt the Islamic religion. Seetzen was known in the east as Sheikh Mussa, or Mussa el-Hakim ("the Doctor"). Burckhardt passed himself off as Sheikh Ibrahim.

However, dressing like Muslims while travelling in the East was not typical only of Seetzen and Burckhardt, for there were other travellers visiting this region at approximately the same time who dressed in the same manner and may have also converted to Islam.

The Arabic disguise of Seetzen and Burckhardt and their perfect knowledge of the Arabic language, customs and religion helped both of them in their researches into the past history and into the cartographical and geographical knowledge of the land. It also brought them close to the people of the country at the time of their visit.

Seetzen's diaries contain enormous material on the towns, villages, roads, agricultural cultivation, people, and other components of the cultural landscape as it was during the first decade of the nineteenth century. Seetzen gives figures on the population of Jerusalem which are accepted today as most accurate. These figures include data on the different religions and sects.

Burckhardt also made a major contribution to the knowledge of the country at the time of his visit. Certainly it is to be regretted that this "most admirable observer of the East" restricted the scope of his travels in the Holy Land. His plans prevented him from visiting the western part of the land. In his determination to avoid the regular routes of his predecessors, Burckhardt purposely stayed away from Jerusalem and Judea, Samaria, the coastal plain and considerable parts of Galilee. However the work he accomplished was very meticulous. His detailed picture of the town of Tiberias, as it looked during his visit, including a small sketch of the walls and other features serve as an example of his thorough work.

The importance of Seetzen and Burckhardt's explorations in the Holy Land, however, is not limited to the fields of study mentioned above. One of the most important achievements of their travels was the great interest in the Holy Land their discoveries aroused. Their scientific approach to exploration inspired many other travellers to follow their lead.

Petra is perhaps the best example of this. The rediscovery of this long-lost city by Burckhardt aroused great enthusiasm and stimulated a wave of followers who attempted to reach the place and explore it. Other subjects such as the way of life of the Bedouins, the rediscovery of their ancient towns, and many additional topics enormously increased the interest in the exploration of the Holy Land.

Without becoming involved in disputes about controversial subjects and dwelling on unimportant details of their adventures, they set aside the former rather fanciful and inexact descriptions of the country and began to lay the foundations for its scientific study.

42

Interestingly, the educations of Seetzen and Burckhardt were very similar. Both studied in Göttingen under the great scholar Professor Johann Friedrich Blumenbach. It seems that the inspiration for their travels came from him, but, more important, their scientific approach probably also originated with Blumenbach.

Seetzen and Burkchardt's publications served as cornerstones of the scientific exploration of the Holy Land.

# IN ARAB DISGUISE — DARING EXPLORERS

James Silk **Buckingham** was a complex and charismatic figure, the subject of conflicting evaluations by his critics. Despite divergent opinions there was little doubt that he was arrogant, vain, and publicity-seeking. More serious charges accused him of plagiarizing Burckhardt and other contemporary travellers.

For example, how is one to take Buckingham's assertion that Seetzen brought about his own death through lack of care? It is difficult to sympathize with a man who blandly asserts that he traversed the length and breadth of the country to a greater extent than any other traveller, and that his journeys to Bashan and Gilead were the first ever made there. But beyond his conceit, Buckingham's books contain valuable material, including surveys, descriptions, facts, and data on the natural and human landscape of Palestine.

Buckingham did not possess the faculty of scientific observation of Seetzen or Burckhardt. He was not a learned man and was unaware of the scientific developments in his own day. Often, his travel notes on the places he visited go off into trite historical tirades without touching on the essence of the subject. Nor does he indicate the sources for his assertions and provides no clue as to how he arrived at his geographical identifications. His evidence and conclusions often negate one another.

Nevertheless, by noting angles of observation, distances, altitudes, and other data, Buckingham contributed to Palestine research and some of this information was used in the compilation of contemporary maps. His book, moreover, contains noteworthy material on the political situation, the gainful occupations of the people, and even on food and dress. Buck-

*Rachel's Tomb, between Jerusalem and Bethlehem. (Buckingham, 1821, II, p. 332).*

At the beginning of the century Rachel's Tomb consisted of one domed room only. It too was a favourite subject of visiting artists, though most of the surviving illustrations are inaccurate. Buckingham filled in the missing parts from imagination. In 1841, Moses Montefiore repaired the building and added an entrance chamber.

44

ingham's writings thus provide an abundance of sketches and anecdotes about life in Palestine, including also many descriptions of the Jews of Jerusalem.

Conceit being Buckingham's outstanding character trait, he tells us much about himself. The lengthy introduction to his book does not skimp on personal details of his life history. Among other things he explains why he went to Egypt, describes his Arab dress, his investigations regarding a possible canal between the Nile and the Red Sea, his meeting with Burckhardt, his illness in Egypt, and his return to England with finds for the London Geographical Society.

Buckingham's writings were published in two books, the first describing his travels after this second visit to Egypt. His aim had been to visit India, but instead he decided to tour Syria and Palestine. In December 1815 he sailed from Egypt to Syria reaching Tyre after ten days at sea. From Tyre he went south to Akko by way of Rosh Haniqra and made Nazareth the base for several journeys. His first book ends with his stay in Nazareth in February 1816, while the second continues the account of his travels from Nazareth to Damascus, Aleppo, and Antioch.

After his travels in the Levant, Buckingham still had an interesting life before him. In 1832 he was elected to Parliament and was active in the anti-slavery movement, thus adding a distinguished chapter to his adventurous past. He travelled about extensively, keeping notes of his many journeys and founded a newspaper in India, but was later expelled for irritating the authorities there. Back in England, he continued editing newspapers and strengthened his social ties with publishers. All these public activities naturally helped to advertise his writings.

Who was **Ali Bey** el-Abbassi? For many years after the death of this traveller-explorer, whose writings give no clue to his true identity, the question puzzled his readers in Europe. More than any of the other travellers of his time, this interesting personality immersed himself in Arab ways and manners so as not to arouse the suspicions of the local population. Unlike Seetzen, Burckhardt, and Buckingham, whose writings revealed their European origins, Ali Bey el-Abbassi persisted in concealing his true identity and religion. For some time it was even conjectured that the man behind the pseudonym was, in fact, Burckhardt. Others suggested that Ali Bey was a Muslim because in one place he writes: ..."Therefore though a Mussulman myself, I must own that the Turks are still barbarians."

45

*Bay of Acre and the Promontory of Mount Carmel — 1816.*
*(Buckingham, 1821, II, p. 113).*

At the beginning of the 19th century Haifa was a small and wretched town. Travellers describe it as surrounded on the inland side by a wall with square towers erected only several decades earlier by the ruler of Galilee, Dahar el-Omar. Through the centre, paralleling the shore, stretched the one and only road with the governor's house at one end. There was a khan full of dirt and mud in the town, and, above it, a small fort with a tower dominated the area. Despite Haifa's small size, Buckingham portrayed it as a town with tall buildings. He also sketched the Carmelite monastery — which at the time of his visit (1816) was abandoned and dilapidated — as rising high above the crest of Mt. Carmel.

46

In the introduction to the English edition the publishers explain that the mysterious traveller had previously published his book in French and that some informed circles in England knew his true origin. And indeed, Ali Bey did go to London to arrange for an English translation. The French writer, Chateaubriand, writes of meeting Ali Bey in Alexandria, but from him, too, the mystery man concealed his real identity.

It later became known that Ali Bey el-Abbassi was a Christian Spaniard named Domingo Badia Y Leblich, who went to seek out a suitable location for a European colony in Morocco. For this purpose he adopted Islam and dressed as an Arab. In 1803 he set out from Spain for Morocco, where he stayed from June of that year until October 1805. He then went on to Tripolitania and Cyprus. Six months later, he arrived in Alexandria and visited Cairo, and Suez. Subsequently, he travelled to Jedda, on the Red Sea coast, and joined a pilgrimage to Mecca, where he arrived in January 1807. He then returned to Cairo, and in July of the same year went on to Jerusalem. A Muslim to all intents and purposes, he visited the Dome of the Rock and made measurements of its interior. In Hebron he visited the mosque above the Tomb of the Patriarchs. Ali Bey also visited Akko, the Carmel area, Nazareth, and by way of Lake Kinneret and the Jordan Valley, Damascus, Aleppo, and Constantinople. Despite his Arab dress and manners, he was stopped between Ramla and Jerusalem by robbers who suspected him of being a Christian. But his knowledge of Arab customs saved him: telling them he had just returned from a pilgrimage to Mecca, he recited passages from the Qoran in proof. Returning from Jerusalem, he encountered the same men, but this time they fell on their faces, wailed, and kissed his feet, having since been told that a certain wayfarer attacked by them was none other than the son of the ruler of Morocco.

Ali Bey el-Abbassi died, apparently during a second journey to Mecca, and was buried at the fortress of Belka, at the crossroads to Mohammed's city. Ali Bey's survey of the country and its conditions are largely superficial; he does not concentrate on antiquities and discoveries. Yet his notes contain some details not found in the writings of other travellers and his measurements were used in the preparation of maps of the country. His journey earned him much praise from Humboldt, the well-known geographer.

Lady Hester **Stanhope** is typical of the European romantics whose long and arduous travels to the Orient were prompted neither by religious

*The Bridge of Jacob's Daughters — 1807. (Ali Bey El Abbassi, 1816, p. 261).*

Most of the sketches in Ali Bey El Abbassi's book are imaginary with little resemblance to reality. One of his less fictitious drawings is that of the Benot Ya'aqov bridge, sketched by him in August 1807.

His illustrated atlas shows a self-portrait in Arab dress and also sketches and cross-sections of the Temple compound in Jerusalem, which he succeeded in visiting, despite the danger were he found to be a Christian.

*The Jordan issuing from the Sea of Galilee. (Mackworth, 1823, p. 296).*

"A Cavalry Officer" was the pseudonym used by the British officer Rigby Mackworth, author of travel books, who visited Palestine in 1821-22 as part of a Middle Eastern tour, after several years in India. His book contains this drawing, interesting in that it shows a relatively large volume of water flowing out of the lake.

49

motives nor by an urge for exploration. For many of them, the assumption of Arab dress was not, as it was for Burckhardt and other explorers, a means of masking their purpose, but an object in itself.

Attracted by the exotic charm of the Orient and captive of their own passionate imaginations, these children of the Age of Romanticism set out to wander amidst the ruins of a glorious past, dreaming of splendid kingdoms lost under the dust of history. Although their activities fall outside the scope of our story, it is impossible not to mention the eccentric Englishwoman who chose to settle permanently in the Lebanese village of Jaune where she died and was buried. Lady Stanhope adopted local masculine attire to avoid having to wear a veil. In 1814 the Sultan granted her a permit to excavate at Ashqelon where, according to rumours, treasure was hidden. True, the site proved rich in "treasure": a Roman marble statue of a man was dug up, but she shattered it and threw the pieces into the sea lest it be claimed that she was searching for artifacts for her country. This act of exhibitionist vandalism was performed in view of the severe criticism of Lord Elgin for taking marble sculptures from the Parthenon to London. There are some who would regard this singular personality as the first woman to excavate in Palestine, but her memoirs, published by her doctor, reveal that she was not at all motivated by a desire to gain knowledge of the country or to explore it. Lady Stanhope's home in Lebanon was for a number of years a "must" for travellers in the region and a meeting place for many explorers.

## THE FIRST TWO DECADES: TRAVELS IN TIMES OF LAWLESSNESS AND INSECURITY

It is not surprising that some of the early travellers should have met. Burckhardt mentions that Lady Stanhope was in Damascus during his visit there; the French politician and author, the Viscount F.A. de **Chateaubriand** met Ali Bey el-Abbassi in Alexandria, during his journey to Greece, Palestine, Egypt, Tunis, and Spain in 1806-1807. The account of this journey is given in three volumes first published in Paris in 1811. Edward Robinson described Chateaubriand's accounts of his travels in Palestine as rhetorical and superficial. This, and similar criticism, does not explain the great success of the work, which went into repeated editions and was translated into many languages. The differences in approach are understandable. Serious explorers who looked to Chateaubriand's work as an aid in their own investigations were put off by the high-flown writing of one who described Palestine as emotionally as had the devout pilgrims of earlier days. On the other hand, the style and contents of the book appealed to those in Europe who wanted adventure stories and lively descriptions of life in the Holy Land, inaccessible to themselves. Chateaubriand considered his work as most accurate. To us its value lies chiefly in some of the realistic descriptions of the country rather than in any methodical research claimed for it by its author. For example, Chateaubriand describes the Church of the Holy Sepulchre as it was two years before the fire that severely damaged it.

"It is a sin and a pity that so much money has been expended on a work so faulty", remarked Titus Tobler, one of the most important 19th century explorers, of a book by another French traveller, the Count Auguste de **Forbin**. Forbin's *Voyage dans le Levant* apparently also appealed to popular taste if not to his learned critics, as is shown by the many published editions. Forbin was a painter, poet, and art historian. After being demobilized from Napoleon's army he became the administrator of the national museums of France and the founder of the Luxembourg Museum. His tours to the Levant took place in 1817-1818. In Palestine he visited many areas, some previously unknown. His notes however, added little to the exploration of the country. Many splendid landscape drawings embellished his book, but they are, unfortunately, largely inaccurate.

As the years went by, more and more travellers who visited the country recorded their impressions in writing. Already in the first two decades of the century such journeys became more frequent, augmenting and enriching the corpus of information.

William **Turner**, author and diplomat on the staff of the British Foreign Office, undertook a five-year journey touring various regions of Turkey and, in 1815, also visited Palestine. To him too, we owe observations on local manners and customs.

In the year 1820, when Turner's book was published in London, the work of a Swiss traveller Johann **Mayr** appeared. He visited Palestine in 1812-1813 and besides descriptions of the country, he gives an extensive survey of Jerusalem.

During Turner's stay, Otto **Richter**, whose work was published posthumously, visited Palestine and, two years later, from 1816 to 1818, Dr. Robert **Richardson** travelled through the Mediterranean and the neighbouring regions in the company of the Earl of Belmore, spending 402 days in Syria, and following the traditional routes in Palestine. Dr. Richardson's work, dealing with only a small area of Palestine, was well-received by many explorers. As might be expected, he noted items of interest to medical men, such as medicinal plants and methods of healing employed by the native population.

A letter dated 7 August 1817, written from Akko by an English traveller, T.R. **Joliffe**, contains notes on his travels in Palestine. This was the first in a series of letters, later collected in book form, giving valuable details and data about the country.

The first modern map of Jerusalem was made in 1818, when the German physician and naturalist, F.W. **Sieber**, reached the city. Noting the inadequacy of the existing plans of Jerusalem, he decided to produce a map based on accurate topographical and geographical data. Choosing 100 precise geometrical points, and using accurate measurements, he pinpointed the city walls, the mosques, the Kidron Valley, and other prominent features of the area. Sieber's map was simpler and more accurate than earlier maps, but it was far from perfect. Neither the city streets nor the valleys outside the walls were drawn correctly. Moreover, he included features that did not exist, and some important buildings were omitted.

Ever since the French invasion, military men have been prominent in the exploration of Palestine, increasing numbers of daring officers coming to the country either individually or as members of research groups.

Captain Henry **Light**, Royal Artillery, obtained a leave of absence from his duties in the garrison of Malta to travel in Egypt, the Holy Land, and Cyprus. Light kept a diary — he was in Palestine in August-September 1814 — and made a number of sketches. Both present a straightforward and interesting record of his tour and effectively convey the atmosphere and conditions in the country. Being an artillery officer, Light kept a sharp eye open for fortified places — Jaffa, Jerusalem, Akko, etc. — and described these and the state of their armaments in the appendix to his published memoirs. But, throughout his travels, Captain Light followed the ordinary routes and did not venture into unknown territories.

Not so, Charles **Irby** and James Mangles, officers in the Royal Navy. Together they travelled in Palestine in 1817-18, at first out of curiosity

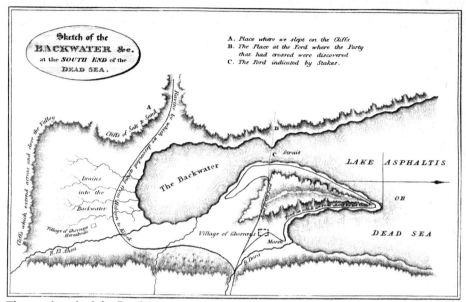

The south end of the Dead Sea — 1818. (Irby and Mangles, 1823, p. 454).

Irby and Mangles's book, in the form of a collection of letters, was first printed in London in 1822 for private circulation. The two British naval officers had been unwilling to publish the letters but were persuaded to do so by friends. In the book is this map of the southern part of the Dead Sea showing the route by which a camel caravan presumably forded the Dead Sea.

and later from a desire to learn the secrets of the country and seek out its antiquities. Disdaining Arab disguise, these self-confident officers moved about boldly as foreigners. They were determined to reach Petra despite the reluctance of their native guides: when these refused to take them there, Irby and Mangles started out by themselves, on foot, and only after they had gone some distance did their escorts rejoin them. They joined Dr. Thomas Legh, and William Bankes, — Byron's friend and Buckingham's one-time travelling companion — in following Burckhardt's route to Petra.

During their nine-months' stay in the country, they usually moved along the regular routes but, in the area east of the Dead Sea, chose unknown paths. Their aims were modest, but their choice of new routes enabled them to add much information. On 1 June 1818, for example, they set out from Kerak to familiarize themselves with the southern part of the Dead Sea. Near the Lashon (Lissan) Peninsula, they met a caravan of pack horses and mules making its way to Hebron and Jerusalem. The merchants, fearing attacks by robbers along the way, implored them not to tell anyone that they had seen the caravan. The following day, arriving opposite the Lashon Strait — the narrowest part of the Dead Sea — they saw to their surprise the same caravan emerging from the water about a kilometre and a half away, ascending the opposite shore. From this they concluded that the Dead Sea at that point was shallow and fordable and that the caravan had passed from east to west through its waters.

In their book, Irby and Mangles include a sketch map of the southern section of the Dead Sea showing where the caravan apparently crossed. This caused many geographers to believe that, in 1818, the Dead Sea level was low enough to be fordable on foot or on horseback. Some explorers construed this to indicate that an ancient route passed through the strait, explaining the location of Massada which overlooks this line of communication.

It is quite possible that the significance of what Irby and Mangles reported has been exaggerated. They were not experienced explorers who thoroughly checked their assumptions. Perhaps it only seemed to them that the caravan emerged from the Dead Sea whereas, in fact, it may have gone round the end of the sea and had not crossed the water at all!

Thomas Legh, one of Irby and Mangles's party, published an article on the journey that mainly consisted of tales and anecdotes of the group's adventures and descriptions of Arab customs. But it was William Bankes, the best-trained and apparently the most outstanding personality of the group, who published nothing. For this he was severely criticized. His admirers praised his modesty of enjoying the journey without seeking publicity. Others, such as Ritter, dubbed him "stubbornly reticent" holding that the advancement of science required a man of Bankes's qualities to reveal to his contemporaries and to future generations what he had learned on his travels.

Did any Jews take part in the exploration of their ancient homeland? The part played by Jews in Palestine investigation in this period was small, for they were then just beginning to emerge from the ghetto. Nevertheless, there were always some Jewish travellers and a few who wrote about their experiences.

Rabbi David **Beth-Hillel** settled in Safed in 1815. Moved by the spirit of travel, he set out on an Oriental tour in 1824, going as far as India in 1832, where, as he says, he was impelled to publish an account of his travels. Five years later, in 1837, he returned home and shortly afterwards became Edward Robinson's guide in Jerusalem. His is the only known travelogue by a Palestinian Jew in the first quarter of the 19th century.

Information about the Jews of Palestine at the beginning of the century, mainly in the four holy cities, Jerusalem, Hebron, Safed, and Tiberias can be gleaned from the letters written by Jewish immigrants from Lithuania, and from the memoirs of local Jewish community leaders of the time.

Of special interest is *Mehkere Eretz Kedumim* ("Researches in an Ancient Land"), published in the Hebrew year 5578 (1818), and concerned with, as the author says "the country's seas, mountains, hills, valleys and so on, including the regions of Palestine and the geographical names mentioned in the Bible." The author was Rabbi Salomon **Löwinsohn** of Prague. In 1839, Jacob Kaplan published a second edition, adding new details of his own. The work is a kind of lexicon of Biblical names of animate and inanimate objects.

*Nazareth. (Wilson, William Rae, 1822, p. 210).*

William Rae Wilson travelled extensively in Palestine, gathering material for his book which appeared in 1823. His landscape illustrations are not very accurate, but do show artistic originality.

At the beginning of the 19th century, Nazareth was a small village of 1,000 to 2,000 inhabitants, mostly Christians, who engaged mainly in agriculture. Wilson's fanciful picture incorrectly shows the town in a depression among the hills. Nazareth had two churches: the Latin Church of the Annunciation near the Franciscan monastery and the Crusader hospice, and the Orthodox Church of the Annunciation near Mary's Well, both outside the village area of those days.

56

*Cana in Galilee. (Wilson, William Rae, 1822, p. 220).*

Wilson was not a military man, but showed daring in embarking on far-flung and often dangerous journeys. He wrote many popular books describing his travels in various lands. In 1819, on his way from Jaffa to Jerusalem, he stayed at the monastery in Ramla that had served as a hostel for Napoleon's sick soldiers. At the village of Abu Ghosh he had to pay the toll levied by the local Arabs before he could continue to Jerusalem.

Kafr Cana is one of the principal sites of Christian tradition. A favourite spot depicted by travellers is the spring with the trough for watering flocks and cattle. Cana suffered severely in the 1837 earthquake, most of its houses being destroyed. Later pictures show new and uncrowded houses spread over a wide area, very unlike typical Arab villages.

# THE THIRD DECADE: MISSIONARIES, SURVEY OF JERUSALEM, THE FIRST GEOGRAPHICAL POCKET GUIDE

In the twenties the number of travellers to Palestine who wrote of their experiences increased slightly but not one of them stands out as an explorer. Among them were several Protestant missionaries whose main interests were not geographical but who gathered much material on Christian religious life in the country. One of the more serious works of this period is that of Johann **Scholz** who visited the country in 1820-1821 and devoted a chapter of the book on his journey to the East to Palestine — its climate, inhabited areas, settlements and everything connected with the Catholic foundations in the land. Scholz knew Arabic well and noted a great number of Arabic place-names.

The missionaries are represented by William **Jowett** and the American Pliny **Fisk**. Both intersperse observations on life in Palestine with discourses setting forth their views on Christianity. Another missionary, Joseph **Wolff**, a converted Jew who visited Palestine twice between 1821 and 1824, wrote several books describing his visit, and his missionary activity in the Holy Land and in other Eastern countries.

The topography of Jerusalem was now beginning to attract the attention of Palestine explorers. The English travellers Frederick **Henniker** and John Carne devoted considerable attention to Jerusalem. Carne wrote two books on his travels in Palestine and the East but was probably better-known for the handsome, illustrated volumes *Syria, the Holy Land, and Asia Minor*, for which he wrote the text. Another traveller, in 1821-2, was John Madox who contributed details of the country's towns and villages, including the Horan region.

Josiah Conder's little book *The Modern Traveller — Palestine*, published in 1825, was probably the first geographical pocket guide-book to Palestine. Summarizing the geographical knowledge of Palestine until about 1823, this work was part of a popular series on the geography, topography, and history of various countries of the world. Conder, who edited the series, explains that because of the extreme importance of Palestine, its topography is dealt with in greater detail than that of other countries. He points to the difficulties in putting together such a book due to the proliferation of source material. Conder expresses the hope that the work will be of use to explorers and adds an appendix of suggested historical and topographical problems future travellers would do well to investigate. In mentioning travellers from whom he collected material, he also passes judgement on their work: Richardson is very exact, mainly with regard to Jerusalem; Ali Bey — interesting details, but not always exact in descriptions; Chateaubriand — better than expected, in particular regarding details on Jerusalem; Clarke — several interesting subjects, but the value of his notes on Palestine seems to be very small in comparison with accounts of his other travels; Buckingham — many thanks for his considerable help and for further details which he personally supplied while the work was in progress; particular gratitude is expressed to Burckhardt and to Irby and Mangles's editor. Conder adds that he gleaned material from Joliffe's letters, Jowett's work, and the travels of Henniker, Captain Light, and Major **Mackworth**.

*The Modern Traveller* volume on Palestine was recognized as a useful compendium by Edward Robinson who included it among the few key books he took with him on his first journey.

But there were also many ordinary men who travelled in these parts and whose adventures and reports awed and fascinated audiences back home. Few went so far as to publish their exploits. Unlike the men of wealth and leisure who formed the majority among the authors of travel books on Palestine in those days, they had no particular social standing and were not sponsored by scientific institutions. Neither were they army officers, clergymen or famous authors, but men driven by a fervent desire to see new landscapes and become acquainted with strange ways of life. Some of these deserve our notice for being unusual personalities in the tribe of globe-trotters.

Such, for example, was the German journeyman-tailor, David **Holthaus**, who travelled the East for sixteen years, visiting Palestine as well. The account of his journeys was first printed in an edition of 1,500 copies which was immediately sold out. Two further editions were produced, the last one when the author was away on his second trip. ·

The value of Holthaus's work lies not only in his well-written and interesting accounts but also in his fresh outlook. He did not travel in comfort

*David Holthaus. (Holthaus, 1841. Frontispiece).*

"I am not an educated man", Holthaus, the German journeyman tailor, tells his readers in apology for his book. His humble purpose in writing, he says, is to recount what befell him during his travels. After 16 long years of travel in distant lands, he returned to a home town that remembered only his name and occupation. When he related his adventures, his entranced listeners pressed him to put them into writing. "Holthaus' book was written by a tailor in honour of all tailors", says his English translator, "for a journey of such extent is unprecedented, and it is as though with his needle he sewed his way from continent to continent". In almost all the countries Holthaus visited he found members of his trade, with whom he worked, earning to pay his way.

60

and was not equipped with letters of recommendation from important people but crossed deserts on foot, made contact with the simple folk, stayed in their homes, lived their grey lives with them, and, through their eyes described the patterns of their lives. On his way to the East, Holthaus passed through Constantinople, where he stayed for about a year and there saved up money for his journey to Egypt via Palestine. It is a pity that only forty pages tell of his travels in Palestine.

Dr. R.R. **Madden** states that his book, a collection of letters sent from the East (Turkey, Egypt, Libya, and Palestine) between the years 1824 and 1827, is about customs and people, not ruins and monuments. A sense of danger runs through all the letters: as a physician he was constantly aware of the perils from diseases endemic in the area.

In Alexandria, Dr. Madden met Moses Montefiore and his wife Judith on their first journey to Palestine in 1827. He addressed some of his published letters to the famous Jewish philanthropist (one was to his wife), and dedicated his book, printed in London in 1829, to him as well.

It was said of the Frenchman Leon de **Laborde**, that he was a diligent traveller and a talented artist. Indeed his beautiful drawings of the ruins of Petra made him famous. These, reproduced as lithographs and woodcuts, form part of a collection of seventy drawings and sketch maps in his book *Journey through Arabia Petraea to Mount Sinai and Petra*, first published as an album in 1830. Most of the drawings (none are of Western Palestine) of the neighbouring regions — Transjordan Sinai, and the Horan — are accompanied by comments extracted by Laborde from the writings of Burckhardt, Henniker, and Irby and Mangles. A splendid edition of the album — the pride of the French publishing trade of those days — was too costly to command a wide public, but in 1836, an English edition was prepared, smaller, easier to handle, and cheaper. The translator added two new chapters: a general report on Idumaea and a summary of observations by earlier visitors to Petra.

George **Robinson**, a visitor in 1830, boasted of his scientific approach despite his lack of training in geography and archaeology. "How easy it is to exaggerate out of emotional excess and how difficult to describe the naked truth", he exclaims, and adds that his attempt to be objective and to keep to facts regardless of his personal opinions should enable his readers to evaluate his work properly.

Just before Mohammed Ali, the Egyptian conqueror, occupied the

*Portrait of Dr. Madden. (Madden, 1829, Frontispiece).*

Madden composed his collection of letters from notes taken during his travels. He usually had to write hurriedly so as not to arouse the suspicion of the local inhabitants. It is perhaps because of their hostility that he dressed in native garb. Here he portrays himself taking the pulse of a native lady-patient fearing for her modesty.

62

country, the Anglican Bishop, Michael **Russell** published a survey of Palestine. His work tried to synthesize geographical descriptions of places with an historical point of view. Russell's topographical descriptions however, concentrate on the holy places. He relies on accounts by contemporary travellers and pilgrims, and recommends the works of Chateaubriand, Richardson, Jowett, Light, Mackworth, Irby and Mangles, Carne, and W.R. Wilson. His book provides a sort of general summary of what was known of the geography of Palestine in his day. In a later edition, in 1850, Russell added details derived from new research.

Like George Robinson and Russell, the Austrian nobleman Anton **Prokesch** describes Palestine before the days of Mohammed Ali. Ritter noted that Prokesch provides much interesting and instructive material on Palestine of the 19th century.

A diary of the years 1821-1841 kept by the Greek priest Neophitus, should not be overlooked. An English translation by Spyridon, published in 1938, is rich in details concerning events in Palestine in the 1820's and 30's, seen from an unusual point of view.

*Mohammed Ali. (Pellé and Galibert, 1840, p. 3).*

The conquest of Syria and Palestine by Ibrahim Pasha ended in the treaty of 1833 by which Syria and Palestine were placed under Mohammed Ali providing he recognised the suzerainty of the Sultan and paid an annual tribute to Constantinople. The ruler of Egypt thus compelled his master to acknowledge the "legitimacy" of his conquest in exchange for the customary tax quota.

The picture is taken from the *Voyage en Syrie et dans l'Asie Mineure*, which is the French version of Carne's *Syria, The Holy Land and Asia Minor*. It is not clear which of the artists who contributed to this volume did the portrait.

64

# CHAPTER TWO

# EGYPTIAN RULE (1831-1840)
# EXPLORATION PERMITTED

*Ibrahim Pasha's encampment near Jaffa. (Carne, 1837, II, p. 30).*

In October 1831, the Egyptian army moved from Cairo to Palestine along the coastal plain. A month later it encamped south of Jaffa, between the town and the tomb of Sheikh Ibrahim al Ajami. At the same time, a fleet under Ibrahim's personal command anchored in the harbour. Faced with this show of force, the town surrendered.

The sky and flags in the picture indicate that it was drawn on a clear, windy day. To the left, on the hill facing the sea, are the staff tents. The soldiers' tents were put up in the vineyards and gardens surrounding the town.

66

# IBRAHIM PASHA:
# CENTRALIZED, EFFICIENT GOVERNMENT

Mohammed Ali's dispute with Abdallah Pasha, the Ottoman governor of Akko provided the pretext for the Egyptian invasion of Palestine in October 1831. One part of the Egyptian forces crossed Sinai, another sailed towards Jaffa. The ancient port town fell to them unopposed, and Jerusalem was taken soon afterwards. But Abdallah fortified Akko and prepared to fight it out.

Ibrahim Pasha, the adopted son of Mohammed Ali, proved to be one of the most gifted commanders of his generation. Even before the Turkish army could organize itself, Ibrahim interrupted the siege of Akko and hurried to meet it, defeating the enemy at the gates of Homs. Akko was subdued on 26 May 1832 after a siege of seven months; the walls were stormed and hundreds of people were buried beneath the ruins. Ibrahim immediately set about its restoration. Damascus and Aleppo were then quickly taken by the Egyptians who crossed the Taurus mountains to confront the hundred thousand-strong main body of the Turkish army under the grand vizir. On 20 December 1832, near Konya, Ibrahim Pasha scored a decisive victory that almost brought the Ottoman Sultanate to an end. It was only the intervention of the European powers, mainly Russia and England, that prevented th collapse of the Ottoman Empire by compelling the Egyptian forces to withdraw.

Ibrahim Pasha remained the ruler of an area that comprised Syria and Palestine, governing it from Damascus. Palestine, its borders reaching to Sidon, became a single district with Jerusalem as its administrative centre.

The success of Mohammed Ali's army under his son's command was due to its comparatively high professional competence and the quality of its equipment. The creation of a modern fleet added to its effectiveness.

During the occupation, Ibrahim Pasha, intent on gaining popular support, dealt considerately with the local inhabitants. He showed particular liberality towards the religious and national minorities. His Christian subjects were protected against excessive taxation and he even extended equality of rights to them. His liberality was exemplified by the permission granted the Jewish community to repair its synagogues. Once his position was consolidated, he initiated administrative changes. With an iron hand, Ibrahim Pasha imposed law and order in towns and rural areas; the Bedouin incursions were curbed and many of these nomads were compelled to settle down; blood feuds between the "Qays" and "Yaman" factions were suppressed; travellers to Jerusalem no longer had to pay road tolls to the people of Abu Ghosh and other local sheikhs; attempts were made to check bribery in the courts and to distribute the burden of taxes more fairly over all sections of the population; new settlements were set up, cultivated areas extended, and trade and industry encouraged.

Yet it was the very introduction of regular, efficient government that provoked dissatisfaction. With less bribe money to pay, people found they could not evade taxes. Banding together against the Egyptian ruler were the Muslim religious leaders who looked askance at Ibrahim's tolerant policy toward the Christians. Men deprived of public office, Bedouin restrained from raiding and pillaging, and, in particular, the fellaheen pressed into military service — all these joined in opposition to the Egyptian ruler. Mass flights of fellaheen to the mountains to escape conscription brought things to a head. Villages were abandoned and fertile areas became desolate, the haunts of thieves and highwaymen. Riot and revolt broke out in the mountain areas around Nablus, in Upper Galilee, Transjordan (Moab and Edom), Hebron, and Bethlehem. In 1834, a widespread uprising broke out, known as "the revolt of the fellaheen." The rebels occupied Tiberias and Safed and besieged Jerusalem, Akko, and Jaffa. Ibrahim Pasha had to call in reinforcements from Egypt and it was only with difficulty that order was restored. The heavy cost of these military actions had to be covered by heavier taxation, fanning yet more disaffection.

Plagues added devastation to the damage done by the revolts. Sanitation being in a deplorable state, and hygienic principles almost unknown, the danger of contagion was high. Victims of cholera, which spread through Upper Galilee in 1838, were thrown into the Jordan River. Moses Montefiore, and others visiting the country in these years, slept outside Jerusalem for fear of contagion.

Towards the end of the 1830's, hostility against Mohammed Ali's government mounted. Even the Maronite Christians in Lebanon seized an opportune moment to rid themselves of the Egyptian yoke. Intending to regain control, the central government in Constantinople began to

68

incite the population against Ibrahim Pasha. In 1839 revolt broke out among the Druse and in its wake a Turkish army invaded North Syria, but defeated by the Egyptians at Nezib, retreated in confusion. It was Ibrahim's intention now to push northwards even though the Ottoman Turks were prepared to come to terms with him. The European powers however, thought differently. England, unable to reach an agreement with France regarding the future of the Ottoman Empire, turned to Prussia and Austria. Mohammed Ali hoped for French aid while on 15 July 1840, England formed an alliance with Russia, Austria, and Prussia for the safeguarding of Ottoman integrity. The decision to oppose Mohammed Ali by force was taken despite opposition by the British representative in Egypt, a friend of the Egyptian ruler, who feared for the fate of the Christians and Jews, and for the future of the holy places should they once again come under control of fanatic Muslims. Mohammed Ali rejected an ultimatum by the powers and British and Austrian warships bombarded and occupied Beirut. Ibrahim withdrew from Syria and moved to defend Akko, but the Allied fleet has already appeared there and Ibrahim prepared for a protracted siege. The fate of Akko was sealed unexpectedly. Shells falling on the main ammunition dump inside the walls caused an explosion that destroyed a large part of the fortifications and claimed many lives. The town was abandoned. The damage was so great that visitors ten years later still described the harbour as a mound of ruins.

Ibrahim Pasha retreated, his army pillaging and burning habitations and fields in their path. Commodore Napier, commander of the Allied fleet, appealed to the populace to throw off Mohammed Ali's yoke, but they used the prevailing chaos for their own ends, creating virtual anarchy. Politically, the war ended in an agreement restricting Mohammed Ali's authority to Egypt and returning Palestine to Ottoman rule.


# SECURITY AND ORDER
# AN INFLUX OF VISITORS


What changes occurred in the country's appearance and how did its inhabitants fare during, and immediately after, the Egyptian occupation? Baron Maria-Joseph de **Géramb**, a Trappist monk, came to the country in 1832 and described what he saw on his travels to Palestine and Mount Sinai. Leaving France in the throes of revolution, he sought a haven near the holy places where he could pursue his beliefs undisturbed. Géramb was one of the first to visit Palestine under Ibrahim Pasha's firm rule and duly noted the greater safety of the roads.

But even then, most travellers kept to the main routes and hurried through the country, missing much they would otherwise have found of interest. There were, however, a few exceptions among them. Edward Hogg M.D. was in the country in 1831-1832, during and immediately after the Egyptian war of occupation and describes events in Akko, Haifa, Jaffa, and Jerusalem. The Reverend Vere Monro and Major T. Skinner toured the country in 1833; their books too, give much valuable information.

"Better what the eye sees than the wandering of desire," as the saying goes; but Alphonse de Lamartine, who as politician and member of the French Academy set out to see for himself the wonders of the magic East, was a prisoner of his own visions. In his highly colourful descriptions poverty and desolation are submerged in splendour and magnificence. For him the radiant majesty of the East, its strange characters and romantic hues cover up unsavoury reality.

Understandably Edward Robinson makes no mention of Lamartine's book. The man who rejected Chateaubriand could not possibly see anything of value in Lamartine's fancies and rhetoric although, in fairness, it must be said that Lamartine himself disclaimed any scientific value for his book.

Robert Curzon, later a Member of Parliament and diplomat, visited Palestine in 1834 in connection with his search for ancient manuscripts in Middle Eastern church and monastery libraries. His reports on various churches, including his description of the deplorable state of the Church of the Holy Sepulchre, raised echoes in the Christian world and were one of the factors that eventually dragged the powers into the Crimean War. His book deals with the provenance and history of the manuscripts and tells the story of how he found them. In addition, it also reviews the Egypt of 1833 and devotes a chapter to Jerusalem and its vicinity.

Another Member of Parliament who visited the Holy Land a year earlier, and wrote an entertaining and witty book about his travels and adventures

*Portrait of Alphonse de Lamartine. (Lamartine, 1835. Frontispiece).*

*Souvenirs, impressions et paysages pendant un voyage en Orient,* was translated into other languages and highly praised for Lamartine's rich, poetic descriptions of the country and his drawings of its splendid views. Nevertheless there is little concrete information about the condition of Palestine beneath the flowery rhetoric.

71

*Bazaar and fountain in Jaffa. (Carne, 1837, II, p. 20).*

During the second decade of the 19th century, a dignitary named Mohammed Agha "Abu Nabut" governed Jaffa and the coastal plain. Abu Nabut restored the ruined city walls and rebuilt the moat. In 1815 he completed the construction of the great mosque of Jaffa and erected a spacious bazaar in the centre of which stood a fountain ornamented with marble slabs and Arabic inscriptions in gold. Parts of the marble bowl still remain but nothing is left now of the canopy and pillars.

Carne, describing this picture, says that the style of the bazaar is more Gothic than Eastern, thus differing from other Oriental bazaars. In the foreground are two Janissaries, a watermelon seller, and Arab women in their native attire.

On the road to Jerusalem, a twenty-minute walk from the east gate in the Jaffa walls, Abu Nabut built another fountain with three large and four small domes, all coloured green. The fountain is still called Sebil Abu Nabut.

*Ancient building in Acre. (Carne, 1838, III, p, 31).*

Carne states that the graceful building known today as Khan el-'Umdan, with its elegant pillars and Gothic arches, stood empty and desolate. With the khan in disuse, the local Franciscan monastery was the only place where foreigners could find lodging. The author states that the monks walked about its compound in idleness, happy at every wayfarer who might bring a little interest into their dull lives.

was Alexander **Kinglake**. *Eöthen* saw many editions — even into the 20th century — being read for its literary style as much as for its geographic interest.

The Duke of **Ragusa** earned renown for his journey through the Balkans and the Levant. Part of his book casts interesting light on the political situation in Syria and Palestine under Ibrahim Pasha. He also made a great contribution to the physical knowledge of the country: his surveying equipment was the best available in his day.

The U.S. Navy ship's chaplain, George **Jones,** who visited Palestine in 1834, describes the changes brought about in Egypt and Syria under Mohammed Ali. They emerged, he says, "from an enshrouding night into the world of light". His commanding officer put at his disposal his own personal diary and a collection of official reports from which Jones drew statistical data that aided him in assuring the accuracy of his survey. He also writes of the fellaheen revolt and of his impressions of Jerusalem and its approach-road from Ramla.

The Swiss doctor Titus **Tobler**, who came to be regarded as the father of German exploration in Palestine, did not suspect, when he set out on his journey to the East in 1835, that he would devote the greater part of his time and energy to the Holy Land.

Doctor, scientist, and sometime politician, Tobler was a supporter of political reform in his homeland. Curiosity about the way different people lived was the motivation for his travels. From Egypt he set out on horseback to Palestine, making his way in five days via El Arish, Rafa, Khan Yunis, Gaza, and Ramla to Jerusalem. After touring the city and its vicinity he went on to Jaffa, whence he sailed for Constantinople.

In his travel diary published in 1839, Tobler regrets that no scientific surveys of Jerusalem were being made. In his opinion neither religious nor secular motives should prevent archaeological excavations or scientific surveys, since "the truth is more holy than all."

"Rivalry between explorers increases knowledge." Tobler, awed by the scope of Robinson's researches, published in 1841, feared that that gifted man had robbed him of his life's ambition. But he soon found rich fields of research for himself in Palestine. He returned to the country a number of times and published other works of great value. These however, belong to a later chapter.

74

# EXPANSION OF GEOGRAPHICAL KNOWLEDGE
# RELIEFS AND TOPOGRAPHICAL STUDIES
# MAPPING OF JERUSALEM

A map of the routes followed by travellers in the first half of the 19th century would show a dense network of lines crossing only certain parts of Palestine like the Akko plain and the mountains of Judea. North or south of the Judean mountains, the lines would become fewer until in Transjordan or in the Negev most areas would remain almost blank. The lack of pertinent topographical data concerning large tracts of Palestine at the beginning of the 19th century made correct and exact mapping impossible. After Jacotin's map was published in 1810, further attempts at mapping the country were made, but in most cases these left much to be desired.

In 1822, J.T. Assheton's map, *An Historical Map of Palestine or the Holy Land*, gained wide circulation. Its large scale (1:350,000) was indicated on the map but despite its technically fine drawing, it reflects none of the great cartographical knowledge of the period. Moreover, in many details it is less exact than Jacotin's map of a dozen years earlier.

Between 1816 and 1820, shortly before the publication of Assheton's map, the Frenchman, Captain Gauthier, carried out a series of measurements along the Syria-Palestine coast, and found that charts based on Jacotin's map showed the coast between Gaza and Haifa Bay almost twenty minutes east of its true location.

The publication of the **Berghaus** Atlas in 1835 marked further progress in the mapping of Palestine. The 1:400,000 scale map of Syria, in the Asia section, is the work of this cartographic artist. Accompanying it is a map of Sinai to a scale of 1:800,000. The Palestine coastline is shown highly indented; deep bays appear near Yavne and Caesarea and, all along the coast, little peninsulas or tongues of dry land protrude into the sea.

In the preparation of his map H. Berghaus used new measurements made by travellers in Syria. He marked administrative units and routes covered by travellers and explorers. For all this, Berghaus's map, too, had its teething troubles and displays a horror of empty spaces. Berghaus did not leave partially or totally unexplored areas unmarked but filled them in with inexact or inconclusive data. In the notes to the map, he explains that although he had assembled authentic material, he also included details of places for which he had no astronomical data or mathematical measurements whatsoever. However, it is hard to believe Berghaus when he says that he filled in the missing details "with the help of his imagination." The notes accompanying his map and explaining his methods are the forerunners of the memoirs to all subsequent important maps of Palestine.

Antedating the Berghaus map were those by Karl von **Raumer** and **J.L. Grimm,** both of which had a Biblical character. The latter, published in 1830, was drawn to a scale of 1:900,000. Gradually travellers became aware of the value of cartography and more accurate and serviceable maps were appended to their books — most of them the work of professional cartographers under the guidance of learned publishers. The "archaic" view of maps as portrayals of the sacred character of the land was still prevalent, but gradually the grip of the past loosened and maps were given new content. The style was still that of Jacotin's map with relief given plasticity by means of hachures and with many level points; but now they were more exact.

It was only in the second half of the fourth decade that a number of explorers discovered almost simultaneously that the major part of the Jordan depression is several hundred metres lower than the Mediterranean. For about ten years, various estimates were made regarding the depth of the depression until, in 1848, Lynch determined the exact level of the Dead Sea.

In the hot month of July 1835, the Irish traveller Christopher Costigan made his way from the Mediterranean to Lake Kinneret by camel caravan, carrying a small boat. With the aid of his Maltese servant he rowed down the Jordan to the southern end of the Dead Sea. At some point, running out of sweet water, he turned back northwards. Suffering severely from thirst under the scorching sun, they made coffee with salt water and eventually reached the northern shore where for a whole day they lay on the ground, exhausted. The servant, with the last of his strength, managed to reach Jericho for help. Burning with fever, Costigan was hoisted onto horseback and taken to Jerusalem where he died in the Latin Monastery. He was buried in the cemetery on Mount Zion.

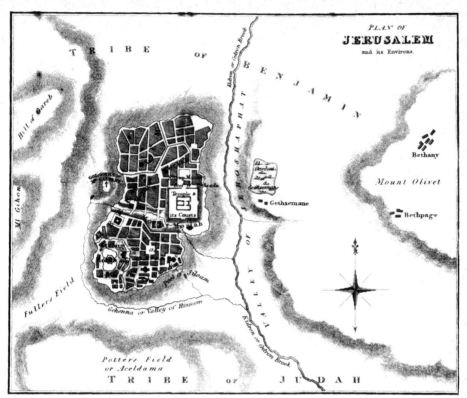

*Plan of Jerusalem. (Wigram, 1837, p. 40).*

Many general books on the Biblical geography of Palestine appeared in the 19th century. One such work, by Wigram included a geographical introduction, an account of
the areas allotted to the Twelve Tribes, and a map of Jerusalem marking Biblical sites
according to identifications advanced by Protestant theologians. This is a typical
example of maps of Jerusalem, combining ancient and modern sites, that were included
in general books up to the middle of the 19th century. Another, similar book was
Graham's *Topographical Dictionary*, listing places mentioned in the Old and New
Testaments alphabetically with reference indications of their location.

77

Although Costigan's purpose was research, he left no notes or reports. But others followed him in studying the Jordan depression, suspecting the existence of a connection between this natural phenomenon and the Gulf of Elat and the Red Sea.

In March of 1837, G.H. **Moore** and W.G. Beke carried a light boat from Jaffa across the Judean mountains to the Dead Sea, intending to explore and survey it. They did not accomplish all they set out to do, but one notable achievement resulted from their journey. Observing the low boiling point of water on the sea shore, they estimated that the Dead Sea level was several hundred metres below that of the Mediterranean. Almost simultaneously, one of the most important explorers of the time — Gotthilf von **Schubert** — arrived at the same conclusion. However, neither he nor Moore and Beke agreed as to the exact level which they placed at between 300 and 350 metres below the Mediterranean. Their calculations were received sceptically. Colonel Camille **Callier**, a well-known French explorer, put the measurement after a survey at minus 200 metres. Further surveys were made the following year, and in 1838 the Count Jules **Bertou** and Joseph **Russegger** came close to the true elevation with 1,300 Parisian feet (419 metres) below sea level.

Three personalities who brought about a turning-point in Palestine research stand out among the explorers of this time. Two of them, Schubert and Russegger, have already been mentioned; the third, Edward **Robinson,** deserves a chapter to himself. Their journeys were undertaken almost concurrently, and their contribution to Palestine exploration includes new finds of immense value.

Although he came to Palestine in 1836-1837 as a biologist, Schubert's interests extended to many other fields. His book is meticulous in all data and details, earning him the respect of the critics. "Schubert has caught the genuine spirit of the East as almost no one of his predecessors has done. ...Without hunting after what is paradoxical, and without losing sight of what is essential and vital... this author...reproduced his own impressions with so much freedom and life, and enriched the mind of his reader... Even where he recounts what is old and trite, his charmingly written narrative finds favour; and everywhere where he undertakes to depict the scenery of the country, he does it with a master's hand." writes George Gage, the English translator of the great geographer Ritter. "Schubert, poet by nature, scholar by training" is the considered appraisal of another critic.

78

Russegger is thought by many to be the pioneer of Palestine geology. An Austrian mining engineer in the service of the Egyptian government, he travelled in the Levant and visited Palestine between the years 1836 and 1838. He was the first to point out the determinant role of limestone in the country's rock structure. Russegger drew up a geological map of the Sinai Peninsula and later published a geological atlas.

In the 30's of the 19th century, Jerusalem was completely unknown from a scientific point of view to the Western civilized world. Maps of the city consisted of nice sketches and drawings of various important buildings but showed complete ignorance of Jerusalem's proper layout or topography. The first modern mapping of the town by Sieber dates to 1818, but was still very primitive.

This pioneer map-making of Jerusalem was carried out under circumstances of great difficulty because the Arabs viewed such work as an act of defilement — a desecration of the holy places through representation. Indeed, surveyors were often threatened by stones and bullets while making measurements on the city walls. Such were conditions until shortly before Catherwood and his party reached Jerusalem in 1833.

Frederick **Catherwood** studied architecture at the Royal Academy in London, and travelled to Rome in 1821, where he joined a group of friends and began painting and making sketches of ancient ruins. In the autumn of the following year he went to Greece — then "the Mecca of architects." Despite revolution and war with the Turks, Catherwood continued his studies there. But when the Turks began an offensive against Athens in 1824, he was finally forced to flee and, with a friend, made his way to Egypt. There, his travels and work with the Robert Hay expedition took him to the ruins of the Nile and their superb monuments — among them those of Karnak, Luxor, and Thebes. At one point he was engaged as an engineer by Mohammed Ali to repair the mosques of Cairo. It was this connection that later enabled Catherwood to enter the el-'Aqsa Mosque and the Dome of the Rock while preparing his survey map of Jerusalem.

Catherwood's work in Jerusalem can be divided into three parts. First, he made a general survey from which he later drew his map. Then, from the roof of the "House of Pilate" and working with his *camera lucida*, he outlined the entire city and sketched each important building. Finally, he concentrated on making a general plan of the Temple Mount and a detailed study of its two sacred places, the Mosque of Omar (the Dome of the Rock) and the el-'Aqsa Mosque. After finishing the general plan and drawings of the exteriors, he entered the mosques and completed plans and architectural details, including an examination of their foundations.

In a rare personal account the architect describes this daring feat in a letter to William Henry Bartlett, who published it in his *Walks About the City and Environs of Jerusalem*.

Dear Sir,
You have asked for some account of my visit to the Mosque of Omar, at Jerusalem, and the ground surrounding it, occupied formerly by the temple of Solomon. You also request my opinion on several points connected with its present topography. I was at Jerusalem in 1833, in company with my friends, Messrs. Bonomi and Arundale, and a portion of my time was employed in making drawings, from which Burford's Panorama was afterwards painted; they were taken from the roof of the governor's house, from whence the best general view of the mosque and its dependencies is obtained. Having so often looked upon the interesting buildings, which now occupy this celebrated spot, I feel (sic) irresistibly urged to make an attempt to explore them. I had heard that for merely entering the outer court, without venturing within the mosque, several unfortunate Franks have been put to death, and you may therefore conceive the attempt was somewhat rash. However, there were many circumstances in my favour; it was the period of the rule of Mehemet Ali in Syria, and the governor of Jerusalem, with whom I was on good terms, was a latitudinarian as to Mahometanism, like most of the pasha's officers. I had brought with me a strong firman, expressly naming me as an engineer in the service of his Highness. I had long adopted the usual dress of an Egyptian officer, and was accompanied by a servant possessed of great courage and assurance, and who, coming from Egypt, held the "canaille" of Jerusalem in the extreme of contempt. This man had strongly urged me to the experiment; and at last, notwithstanding the remonstrances of my friends, I entered the area one morning, with an indifferent air, and proceeded to survey, but not too curiously, the many objects of interest it presents. As I was about to enter into the mosque, however, I caught sight of one of the guardian dervishes, who are in the habit of conducting pilgrims around it; this man made towards me, in the hope of a better donation than usual. As I was not prepared to go through the requisite ceremonial with this devout guide, I thought it prudent to retreat, as if accidentally, from his alarming neighborhood, and quietly left the area, without having occasioned the least notice. The success of my first attempt, induced me to make a second visit the following day. I determined to take in my camera lucida, and sit down and make a drawing; a proceeding certain to attract the attention of the most indifferent and expose me to dangerous consequences. The cool assurance of my servant, at once befriended and led me on. We entered, and arranging the camera, I quickly sat down to my work, not

80

without some nervousness, as I perceived the Mussulmen, from time to time, mark me with doubtful looks; however, most of them passed on, deceived by my dress and the quiet indifference with which I regarded them. At length, some more fanatic than the rest, began to think all could not be right: they gathered at a distance in groups, suspiciously eyeing me, and comparing notes with one another; a storm was evidently gathering. They approached, broke into sudden clamour, and surrounding us, uttered loud curses: their numbers increased most alarmingly, and with their numbers their menacing language and gestures. Escape was hopeless; I was completely surrounded by a mob of two hundred people, who seemed screwing up their courage for a sudden rush upon me — I need not tell you what would have been my fate. Nothing could be better than the conduct of Suleyman, my servant, at this crisis; affecting vast indignation at the interruption, he threatened to inform the Governor, out-hectored the most clamorous, and raising his whip, actually commenced a summary attack upon them, and knocked off the cap of one of the holy dervishes. This brought matters to a crisis; and, I believe, few moments would have passed ere we had been torn to pieces, when an incident occurred that converted our danger and discomfiture into positive triumph. This was the sudden appearance of the Governor on the steps of the platform, accompanied by his usual train. Catching sight of him, the foremost, — those I mean who had been disgraced by the blows of Suleyman — rushed tumultuously up to him, demanding the punishment of the infidel, who was profaning the holy precincts, and horsewhipping the true believers. At this the Governor drew near, and as we had often smoked together, and were well acquainted, he saluted me politely, and supposing it to be beyond the reach of possibility that I could venture to do what I was about without warrant from the pasha, he at once applied himself to cool the rage of the mob. "You see, my friends," he said, "that our holy mosque is in a dilapidated state, and no doubt our lord and master Mehemet Ali has sent this Effendi to survey it, in order to complete its repair. If we are unable to do these things for ourselves, it is right to employ those who can; and such being the will of our lord, the pasha, I require you to disperse and not incur my displeasure by any further interruption." And turning to me, he said, in the hearing of them all, that if any one had the hardihood to disturb me in future, he would deal in a summary way with him. I did not, of course, think it necessary to undeceive the worthy Governor; and gravely thanking him, proceeded with my drawing. All went on quietly after this.

During six weeks, I continued to investigate every part of the mosque and its precincts, introducing my astonished companions as necessary assistants in the work of survey. (Mr. Bonomi, speaking Arabic fluently, had found no difficulty in entering the mosque on several previous occasions, but the character he assumed, of a Mahomedan pilgrim, had hitherto precluded his making drawings.) But when I heard of the near approach of Ibrahim Pasha, I thought it was time to take leave of Jerusalem. The day after my departure, he entered, and as it happened, several English travellers of distinction arrived at the same time. Anxious to see the mosque, they asked permission of Ibrahim, whose answer was characteristic of the man, to the purport, that they were welcome to go if they liked, but he would not insure their safe return, and that he could not venture to outrage the feeling of the Mussulmen, by sending an escort with them. Here he was met with the story of my recent visit. He said it was impossible: the dervishes were summoned; the governor was summoned, and an eclaircissement took place, which must have been a scene of no small amusement.

It was more than simple curiosity that urged this rash attempt, and its fortunate issue enabled me, with my associates, to make a complete and scientific survey of the mosques, vaults, gateways, and other objects comprised within the extent of the area. These I hope, at some future period, will be published.

Three maps of Jerusalem of different scales resulted from Catherwood's efforts, one published in 1835, the other two copyrighted in 1838. Today, Catherwood's maps are considered among the most accurate of the early survey maps of the Holy City. But perhaps of greater significance are his drawings of important sites in Jerusalem, some of which, like that of the Dome of the Rock and the interior of the Golden Gate, appeared as illustrations on his largest map.

Catherwood's drawings of Jerusalem were never published in book form as he had intended. When London publishers showed no interest, he filed his drawings away. But over the years some were published individually. They have become known mainly because other painters and travellers used Catherwood's original sketches to make drawings of their own. Probably the most familiar of these are found in Thomas H. Horne's two-volume *Landscape Illustrations of the Bible.*

That relatively little remains of Catherwood's work in Jerusalem is due in large measure to the architect's generosity in helping to solve an academic dispute. In 1847, when James **Fergusson**, the architecture historian, asked Catherwood for his drawings in an effort to prove his theory that the Dome of the Rock had been built by Constantine over the tomb of Christ, Catherwood turned them over to him. And then they disappeared.

Fortunately, the map of Jerusalem fared somewhat better. Its service to other scholars who studied the city is well documented. Heinrich Kiepert, who made several maps of Jerusalem and the Holy Land, points out that in all details relating to the Temple Mount, the most correct and complete map is that of Catherwood. In his memoir on the maps in Robinson's work, Kiepert explains: "As the measurements of Robinson and Smith did not contain material enough for the construction of an entirely new plan of the Holy City, they could be employed only for correcting and

*Convent of the Cross, Jerusalem. (Bartlett, 1855. p. 190).*

"One of the most pleasant spots within a short distance of Jerusalem is the Convent of the Cross. It is seen on the right approaching the city by the Jaffa road, prettily retired in a valley," writes Bartlett in his *Jerusalem Revisited*. During his first visit he found only three monks in the monastery, but when he returned twelve years later, he saw a school for Greek Orhodox boys, established there four years previously, with ninety pupils and four teachers, and a curriculum of classical Greek, German, French, geography, and arithmetic.

According to Bartlett, the monastery is the last remnant of ancient Jerusalem's Orthodox Georgian church, whose influence in the past had been great. Local Christians believe that the wood for the Cross was taken from this site. In the church a hole is shown where grew the tree from which the Cross was made.

completing the best of the plans already extant, viz. that of Catherwood, which has been adopted as a basis." Robinson himself found Catherwood's unpublished drawings most valuable, for he often cites them and credits the architect for information included in his description of Jerusalem.

According to another 19th-century historian, George Williams, Catherwood's map was the standard plan of Jerusalem from its publication in 1835 until 1849.

Valuable as the publication of the map of Jerusalem was to scholars and cartographers of the period, it was of particular consequence to Catherwood himself, for it had a profound effect on his career. It served to introduce him to John Lloyd Stephens, who, while travelling through the Levant, "was fortunate to find a lithographic map made by Mr. Catherwood," which he says was "a better guide to all the interesting localities than any other (he) could procure in Jerusalem."

Frederick Catherwood, "architect-explorer of two worlds" became well-known for his work with John Lloyd Stephens in Central America, particularly the Yucatán. Of his drawings of their explorations of the Mayan civilization, much remains. Of his work in the Old World — the Middle East — little has survived.

John Lloyd **Stephens**, signing his books "An American Traveller", was a lawyer whose extensive travels took him through many parts of the world. His *Incidents of Travel in Egypt, Arabia Petraea, and the Holy Land* describing his unusual journey, in 1836, in a lively narrative style, quickly became popular and was reprinted many times over. Stephens was the first self-acknowledged tourist — as distinct from the explorers — to enter Palestine by way of Eastern Sinai, Aqaba, Petra, and Hebron. His book enticed many others to follow in his footsteps.

Catherwood and Stephens, who joined together later in exploring parts of Central America, exemplify the great interest in travel and exploration of an age intent on eliminating all the remaining places on the world map, marked "unknown", or "unexplored". It is also interesting to note that despite the primitive methods of communication, travellers managed to meet and to know of one another.

Catherwood's travelling companion, F. **Arundale**, also published a handsome illustrated volume, containing a map of Jerusalem, and giving

84

details of the Temple Mount. But it is far less important than the work of his friend.

# EDWARD ROBINSON: THE FOUNDATION OF PALESTINE EXPLORATION

When Edward **Robinson** was offered the chair of Biblical Literature at the Union Theological Seminary in New York, he stipulated that he first make a tour of the Holy Land. His journey, undertaken in 1838, realized a childhood dream. The fruit of this first visit, the *Biblical Researches in Palestine, Sinai, Arabia Petraea and Adjacent Regions*, published in 1841 in both English and German, earned him the gold medal of the Royal Geographical Society. The work was enthusiastically received by geographers and Bible scholars. The German edition, translated partly by himself and partly under his supervision, was dedicated to the German geographer Carl Ritter whom Robinson regarded as his mentor and teacher.

Robinson's researches opened the way to new topographical and historical discoveries and basically changed geographical knowledge of 19th century Palestine. He was assisted by his pupil and friend, Eli Smith, who accompanied him in Palestine. Orientalist, linguist, student of theology and former missionary in Malta and Beirut, Eli Smith was at home in the Arab world and could thus gather much valuable information that was inaccessible to other explorers. Over the years, Smith collected the names of places in the country he one day hoped to visit, in an attempt to identify them with sites known from tradition or determined by earlier explorers.

Robinson attributes much of the success of his travels to Eli Smith who collaborated fully in all the investigations. Each kept his own diary separately so that they could later compare notes and evaluations. The diaries served as the basis for Robinson's published work. Robinson prepared himself for his journey by going through all the accessible literature on Palestine with rare diligence and perseverance, collating every bit of information on file cards. The vast amount of material he accumulated served as an indispensable compendium for students of the Biblical geography of Palestine.

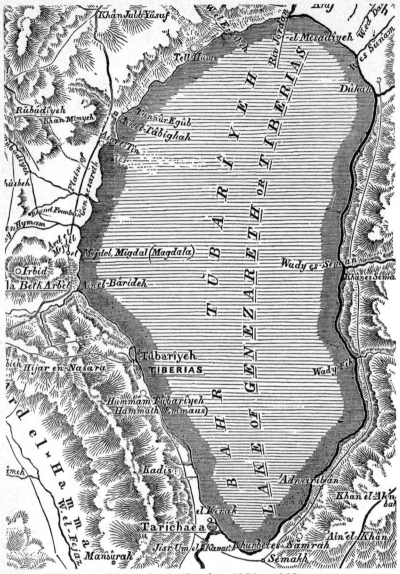

*Lake of Tiberias and its environs. (Stanley, 1856, p. 360).*

The map is from the first edition of Robinson's *Biblical Researches*. Although the Berghaus map was used by Edward Robinson, he soon realized that its inaccuracies would hinder his work. From his own findings he made new maps that became a turning-point in the cartography of Palestine. The map of the Sea of Galilee is an example of this explorer's work.

*Portrait of Dr. E. Robinson. (Conder, 1889, Plate 16).*

Theologian, linguist, professor of Biblical literature at the New York Union Theological Seminary, and explorer, Robinson examined Biblical sites scientifically, discarding fanciful traditions. Previous explorers, and especially Schubert, studied the physical characteristics of the country; he therefore directed his attention to its Biblical-geographical aspects, in particular, to the correct locations of the holy places.

87

The great success of Robinson's first journey may be ascribed to the combination of his knowledge of the geography and history related to the Scriptures, and Eli Smith's wide experience of the language and customs of the country. Their joint work became the foundation of later Palestine exploration and stimulated other explorers of stature to devote themselves to the region.

In his books Robinson dwells on two main shortcomings of his predecessors, and in so doing clarifies his own basic approach. Whether Catholic or Protestant, the explorers relied for their information on the monks of the monasteries they lodged in, who acted as their guides. Their reports were thus stereotyped, since traditions based on legend and folklore preserved within the churches and the Catholic orders in the Holy Land were transmitted from generation to generation without any scientific re-examination. Most travellers simply embodied them in their writings without bothering, or being able, to check the origins of these traditions.

The other failing was their ignorance of Arabic that precluded any first-hand communication with the local population without an interpreter. Moreover, not knowing the language of the country, most travellers felt insecure and kept to the main roads. Because of all this, their observations were limited in scope.

Robinson and Smith took to side roads besides following the main pilgrim routes; there is hardly a Biblical site west of the Jordan they did not visit.

Aware of the Arab's habit of giving answers to please the questioner, they only conducted general conversations with Arabs and did not ask for direct answers. Thus they obtained the information they sought without fanciful supplements.

While analyzing place names, they confirmed the conclusion reached by Seetzen and Burckhardt that later traditions which grew up under Greek and Roman influences had to be distinguished from the earlier Semitic ones preserved by the local population.

Robinson and Smith readily admitted that the first to understand the great significance of the Arabic place names had been Seetzen and Burckhardt. These however had compiled a list for Palestine east of the Jordan, no one having as yet done so for Western Palestine. Robinson and

Smith gathered names of villages and ruins by questioning the local people. From Jerusalem and Gaza they toured the surrounding villages, even spending time in Bedouin tents. They visited the monasteries only after they had finished collecting their material in order to compare it with the legends and traditions of the monks.

Two pocket-compasses, a thermometer, telescope and a measuring tape; an English and Hebrew Bible, the works of Reland and Raumer on Palestine, the reports of Burckhardt and Laborde, Conder's *The Modern Traveller* volume on Palestine and Arabia, Berghaus's map, Laborde's map of Sinai and Arabia Petraea — this was the "scientific" equipment they took on their travels. On his second visit, Robinson included Ritter's important work.

Their camping gear was even more modest. Robinson, Smith, and the cook rode on horseback; mules carried their servant, tent, bedding, and food supplies. Not an hour of their journeying passed without their noting observations, and every night they wrote up their notes. Robinson stressed the importance of making frequent notes and deplored Burckhardt's practice of delaying sometimes as much as two whole days before writing down what he saw and heard. To their great satisfaction Robinson and Smith found that the notes they took independently corresponded to a remarkable degree. These notes proved so interesting that, at the insistence of their friends, they included them, in addition to their conclusions, in the account of their travels.

Robinson considered the main roads to have been amply explored. The Jordan depression too, seemed to him no longer unknown, for a year earlier the extent of the rift and the level of the Dead Sea had been studied. Since knowledge of the Jordan Valley and its vicinity was by then quite advanced, Robinson decided to turn his attention to lesser-known areas.

Setting out on 12 March 1838 from Cairo to Sinai, they reached the Negev — a region as yet hardly penetrated — and discovered some of its ancient cities, devoting special attention to the extensive ruins of Halutza. (Later, they also travelled in the Arava and visited Petra and its vicinity.)

From Beer Sheva they went on to Hebron and Jerusalem and, after a tour of Judea, continued through Nazareth and Tiberias to Beirut. They had spent only two and a half months in Palestine, and their entire journey since leaving Egypt had taken less than four months. But despite its relative briefness, the results of the journey greatly surpassed their expectations.

Robinson planned his routes to recross from time to time. In this way he could confirm over one thousand site locations he determined by compass, by reaching them from different directions. He also made measurements of the length and breadth of the Dead Sea. For technical reasons, and because he only had a compass, his calculations were inexact; they were however, closer to the truth than any of the currently accepted estimates.

Edward Robinson's guiding principle was that the study of Palestine required understanding of the interrelations between the physical setting and its historical development. Therefore, after his second journey, this approach coloured all his subsequent studies of the country. Even on his first visit he had not limited his investigations to any one field; he copied out Greek inscriptions and noted details of all kinds that seemed important for a first acquaintance with the country. Nevertheless his writings contain some serious errors. Robinson was not very familiar with archaeological material from Mesopotamia and did not understand the significance of tels. This caused him to miss historically important places such as Tel El-Hesi, Tel Lakhish, and the huge artificial mound of ancient Jericho. On the other hand, he must be credited with several valuable archaeological discoveries: in Jerusalem he explored, among other sites, the Siloam tunnel; discovered the spring of the arch south of the Wailing Wall — it is still known as Robinson's Arch — and found the remains of the third wall built by Agrippa. In Galilee he identified synagogues, including that of Capernaum, and in the Negev, investigated ancient Byzantine cities in ruins since the early Arab era; in Edom, his attention was given to Petra and the ruins in its vicinity.

Robinson's book is a cornerstone of 19th century Palestine exploration: whoever wished to understand the Palestine of that period had to follow him along its highways and byways.

His low opinion of the Latin monastic orders as represented in the country, and his scepticism concerning their traditions and legends earned him much criticism. In some cases, such as that regarding the Church of the Holy Sepulchre, his views were extreme, but always stemmed from his uncompromising desire to uncover the truth. Robinson did not see his work as complete and, out of a strong sense of self-criticism, did not hesitate to admit not knowing something. He considered his first journey as only the beginning of his explorations and, returning ten years later in 1852 for another visit, set himself new goals. But on the other hand, he did not always take kindly to criticism by others and at times exhibited an almost unreasonable obstinacy in defending his site identifications.

From the outset Robinson displayed remarkable ability and stamina. Setting out one day at 2:15 after midnight from Dahariya, he reached Jerusalem at six o'clock in the evening — sixteen hours on camelback! At nine o'clock the next morning he was already at the entrance of the Church of the Holy Sepulchre. No wonder, therefore, that after four months of continuous effort he fell ill. Illness likewise ended his second journey. He died on 27 January 1863 aged 69. Though he was unable to carry out all his plans, he is unanimously regarded as the most important explorer of Palestine in the 19th century.

Robinson and Smith also made a significant contribution to the cartography of Palestine. The routes they travelled and the details they gathered were plotted on large-scale plans that were used in the preparation of the maps attached to their books. The *Biblical Researches* contain a general map of Palestine to a scale of 1:800,000 in two sheets, and two maps scaled 1:100,000 of Jerusalem and the presumed site of Mt. Sinai. The maps were prepared by Heinrich **Kiepert,** a well-known German cartographer, from data supplied by Robinson and Smith. Thousands of triangulations and details gathered by them, despite the lack of exact astronomical measurement, were carefully worked over by Kiepert. Only five years after Berghaus's map appeared, Robinson and Smith had already assembled enough material for a new one — although there was nothing new to add to the eastern side of the Jordan. There is no doubt that the general conditions of security prevailing under Egyptian rule allowed Robinson and Smith to investigate places that their predecessors had found too dangerous.

Kiepert also drew other maps besides those included in Robinson's book and, in 1842, published a general map of Palestine, to a scale of 1:600,000. This was so well received that a second edition followed a year later with the eastern part of Palestine redrawn from data not available previously to Berghaus.

*Jaffa, looking south. (Carne, 1837, II p. 38, Bartlett).*

Jaffa at the turn of the 18th century was a walled city built on a hill facing the sea. Napoleon breached the walls, but later repaired them, only to destroy them again when he retreated. The city was rebuilt and embellished by its Ottoman governor, Abu Nabut. A fortress crowned the hill, while its bustling market occupied a long street in the lower town. Outside the walls was the Muslim cemetery, which, the text explains, differed from other Oriental burial grounds in that it was bare of greenery and plants.

92

*Jaffa, looking south. (Roberts, 1842, p. 58).*

Roberts's book *The Holy Land* immediately attracted attention, because of the delicacy of his drawing and its elegant style. This picture of Jaffa was made from the same point as the preceding illustration by Bartlett. It is interesting to compare the two. According to the artist, the figures in the foreground are Jewish pilgrims from Poland just returned from Jerusalem, awaiting a ship to take them back to Europe.

# THE SUPERB ILLUSTRATORS:
# DAVID ROBERTS AND OTHERS

The Scottish painter, David **Roberts,** raised a flurry of excitement and wonderment among people interested in the Holy Land when he exhibited his drawings of places in the Near East and the Holy Land. A selection of lithographs made from his many sketches was published in three elephant-folio volumes between 1842 and 1846. It was the most comprehensive pictorial record of the buildings and scenery of this region in the early Victorian period. The first volume shows landscapes and sites in Jerusalem, Galilee, the Jordan, and Bethlehem; the second is of Idumea, Petra, Egypt and Nubia, and the third also of Egypt and Nubia. Later editions appeared in various formats. Roberts began his career by designing theatre sets, but was then drawn to paint landscapes. His growing reputation led to commissions to paint subjects from many countries, including the Holy Land. At first he worked from travellers' descriptions, but after a visit to Spain and Morocco was moved to see Palestine for himself. Drawings brought back from the East by the French commission that accompanied Napoleon being regarded in Europe as unsatisfactory representations, Roberts was asked to visit the same places. Equipped with letters from the Foreign Office, he left London on 31 August 1838. His first stop was Alexandria where he was assisted by the British Consul-General who also arranged for official permission to visit the mosques. In Egypt he made drawings of ancient sites that appealed to him. At first intending to set out for Palestine, via El Arish and Gaza he was induced to change his itinerary after seeing the original drawings of Petra of the Laborde expedition. His curiosity aroused, Roberts decided instead to cross the Sinai Desert to Aqaba, and then go on to Petra and Hebron.

Roberts and his companions, Pell and Kinnear, adopted Bedouin dress. Their party consisted of several armed servants and Bedouin guides and camel drivers. On 27 February 1839, after a nine or ten-day journey, they reached Aqaba where other Bedouins took over responsibility for their safety as they had passed outside the area of jurisdiction of their original guides. At the beginning of March they reached Petra. There they

94

*The Tower of David. (Roberts, 1842, p. 7).*

Roberts' sketches on the whole faithfully portray the country's landscapes and places of interest, and the architecture of its ancient structures. Although his work is infinitely more accurate than earlier drawings, he inclines to idealization, his drawings often seeming to improve on reality. He often adds human figures to his pictures in order to make his work more interesting and attractive.

David's Tower — the citadel of Jerusalem — its large ashlars, surrounding moat, and its overall monumentality was a popular subject with 19th century travellers. These tell us that entrance to the citadel was forbidden to pilgrims and that the building, containing a number of cannons, housed the Turkish garrison of Jerusalem.

*Ramla. (Roberts, 1842, p. 66).*

At the beginning of the 19th century Ramla was an open town, its former walls having disappeared. In size it approximated Jaffa, though its houses were not as crowded together. The population of Ramla was about 3,000 — of which one-third Greek Orthodox and Armenian Christians. Their main source of income came from agriculture: cereal grains, olives, and cotton, as well as from small-scale production of soap and pottery. As the town stood at a junction of roads of the coastal plain, and to Jerusalem and the South, it contained a central khan. A number of Catholic monks resided in the Latin monastery, one of the largest in the country, that, since the 18th century, served as a hospice for Christian pilgrims. Some of Napoleon's soldiers also rested one night within its walls. Roberts visited the town and the monastery, the monks showing him the White Tower in the compound of the ruined mosque, which they claimed were the remains of a church. Roberts expressed his doubts, the architecture being clearly Saracen.

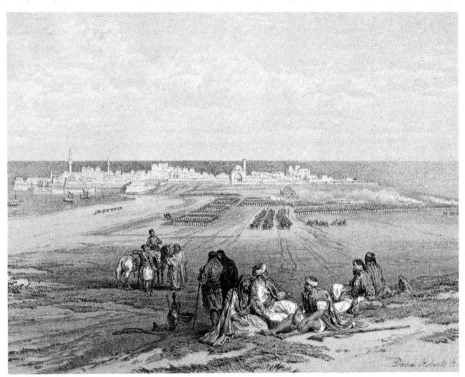

*St. Jean d'Acre. (Roberts, 1842, p. 63).*

In the space of forty years Acre suffered in three major battles: Napoleon's abortive attempt in 1799, Ibrahim Pasha's conquest in 1832, and its recapture by the Turkish and British forces in 1840. Of the three, the last one was the most destructive. Roberts visited Acre in 1838 before its destruction, but his work was published after the year 1840. He probably completed his sketch by taking into account the siege and the results of the bombardment.

97

*Haifa, looking towards Mt. Carmel. (Roberts, 1842, p. 60).*

In 1838, a sailing vessel neared the coast of Palestine, carrying Jewish immigrants from Morocco intending to settle in Galilee. The boat was wrecked and twelve of its passengers drowned. The survivors eventually settled in Jaffa. Apparently moved by the disaster, Roberts drew the wrecked ship, adding a note on the treacherous nature of the coast.

Haifa, appears here more exactly drawn than in earlier illustrations. (Compare Buckingham, p. 46). Roberts carefully distinguished the various parts of the town: the ancient walled section, the "Burj" — the fortress commanding the area, the minaret of the mosque, and the Carmelite monastery on the Carmel overlooking the sea.

98

remained for several days unable to tear themselves away from the wonders of the abandoned city. In Hebron, they found the way to Jerusalem closed because of the plague. They therefore turned off to the coastal route, via Gaza, Ashqelon, and Jaffa, and reached the Holy City on 29 March, by which time conditions there had improved. The governor of Jerusalem arranged for Roberts and his companions to join a party of 4,000 pilgrims from the Eastern churches going to Jericho and to the traditional place of baptism on the Jordan. Having feasted his eyes on the Dead Sea and the Jordan Valley, they continued northwards to the mountains of Samaria, Lake Kinneret, the mountains of Lebanon, Baalbek, and the Mediterranean coast. Illness prevented him from going further into Syria and to Palmyra.

John **Kinnear**, who accompanied Roberts, dedicated the book he wrote on their journey, *Cairo, Petra and Damascus in 1839 with remarks on the Kingdom of Mohammed Ali and the present situation in Asia*, to the artist.

Shortly after Roberts, in 1841 the famous painter David **Wilkie** toured the country. His album — the original paintings are in the British Museum — contains twenty-six portraits. Among his subjects are Mohammed Ali, Sultan Abdul Majid, a sheikh — his body-guard on the journey to the Dead Sea, and Jewish women.

Other artists of the 1830's depicted the country from other viewpoints. Bearing the title *Landscape Illustrations of the Bible consisting of views of the most remarkable places mentioned in the Old and New Testaments*, a collection of 32 illustrations based on sketches made by travellers, was published in 1835. The pictures, superbly engraved by W. and E. Finden, had an explanatory text by the Reverend Thomas **Horne**, their editor. At the bottom of each picture are the name of the artist and of the traveller who made the original sketch. David Roberts was one of the artists represented; his drawings here were made before he had visited the country. A second edition, a year later, contained additional illustrations.

J.M. **Bernatz**, touring in 1837, depicted the landscapes and sites of Palestine. His first book, published in 1839, shows Biblical sites such as Hebron with the building over the Tomb of the Patriarchs, Bethlehem, Mount Tabor, the Tower of David, Jerusalem, and the Temple Mount. Another edition published in 1855 and entitled *Album des heil. Landes* contained new pictures with a commentary in English, German, and French. Some of these pictures are in colour and several are of particular

*Tiberias before the 1837 earthquake. (Lindsay, 1838, p. 262).*

interest: scenes of the Temple Mount, prayers at the Wailing Wall, the village of En Karem, Shekhem, Kafr Cana, Safed, and the Benot Ya'aqov Bridge over the Jordan. Bernatz's pictures were repeatedly copied in other books published during the century.

The French painter Adrien Dauzats preceded Bernatz and others mentioned in this chapter. He visited the Levant in 1830 and with the aid of the novelist Alexandre **Dumas**, who apparently did not himself visit the country, wrote *Quinze jours au Sinai.* His drawings were used subsequently in a number of books — mainly in the work by Baron Isidore **Taylor** and Louis Reybaud, *La Syrie, l'Egypte, la Palestine et la Judée,* which appeared in France in 1839. He depicted the market place of Akko, the Jewish and Christian quarters of Jerusalem, the Tomb of Christ, David's Tower, the Damascus Gate, the Pool of Siloam, the entrance to the Tombs of the Kings, Christians in Bethlehem, a building in Gaza, the interior of the Church of the Annunciation in Nazareth, the Jubb Yusif Khan in Upper Galilee, remains of a temple and Roman theatre in Amman, Bedouin guards in a Sinai caravan, and Jaffa from the sea.

100

*Tiberias after the 1837 earthquake. (Lindsay, 1838, p. 262).*

Visiting Palestine in 1835-1836 was the Russian Minister of Public Education, Abraham von **Noroff**, who knew Arabic and other Semitic languages. He too produced a book about his travels which appeared in 1838. His diary kept during a second journey, in 1861, this time including also Sinai, was published in 1878 in St. Petersburg under the title *Jerusalem and Sinai.*

The Vicar C.B. **Elliot** describes the way of life and customs of the peoples among whom he travelled in *Travels in the Three Great Empires of Austria, Russia and Turkey* (1838). He was accompanied by J. Nicolayson, a Church of England missionary, who lived many years in Palestine and who supplied him with information about the Bedouins and the fellaheen as well as about Ibrahim Pasha. Elliot offers some new and interesting facts, but his descriptions are too general and contain many mistakes.

In 1837 an earthquake in Galilee caused much devastation and heavy loss of life. The catastrophe gravely affected the Jewish communities of Safed and Tiberias.

Naturally, most travellers' accounts of the years immediately after 1837

101

mention this event and its sad effects. J.N. Visino, an Austrian army chaplain, J.D. **Paxton,** Lord **Lindsay,** and others describe the devastation in Tiberias and Safed. The much-travelled Prince **Pückler-Muskau,** from Silesia, suggested to Haim Weisman, his Jewish guide in Galilee, that he put up a hotel in Tiberias facing the lake.

Joseph Salzbacher, from Vienna, arrived in the same year. Apart from an historical account, he describes the condition of the Catholic institutions in Palestine.

Notable among the missionaries active in Palestine in this period are Andrew **Bonar** and Robert McCheyne. They were sent by the Church of Scotland to ascertain the possiblities of converting Jews. Their book provides important material about the inhabitants of the country.

Among other visitors before the return of the Turks are several Americans: Stephen **Olin,** who wrote a sensitive and highly intelligent account of his travels that was appraised as second only to Robinson's; and James E. **Cooley,** who was in Egypt in the years 1839-1840 and whose book *The American in Egypt with Rambles through the Holy Land*, dwells mainly on aspects of Egyptian rule.

The new interest in the region evoked by Mohammed Ali's conquest resulted in numerous books on the geo-political situation, special attention being directed to the Druse and Maronites of the Lebanon. Among these books were works by C.G. Addison and C.H. Churchill.


# PRELUDE TO JEWISH REVIVAL IN PALESTINE: MONTEFIORE'S SECOND VISIT


Moses **Montefiore** visited Palestine seven times, but his second visit, in 1839, was of particular importance. Concluding that charitable donations did not provide long-term solutions, he decided to devote himself to improving the condition of the Jewish population in a more permanent way. In this he was actively assisted by Eliezer Halevi, his secretary for twenty-five years. This learned man had already visited Palestine in 1838 in the course of an extensive Eastern journey, describing his impressions in letters from Safed, Nablus, Jerusalem, and Hebron. At

102

Montefiore's request, he conducted a census of the Jewish population preliminary to a comprehensive programme for their advancement. Montefiore's desire to encourage the Jews to live by their own productive labour did eventually result in some of them starting settlement projects.

Against this background, attempts at setting up agricultural settlements were made by some Jews of Safed. The man who became the first Jewish farmer of modern times in the ancient Land of Israel was Rabbi Israel Bak. After coming to Safed from Poland in the 1820's, he set up a printing-press but it turned out to be unprofitable. He appealed to Ibrahim Pasha, then in Akko, for the grant of a plot of land for cultivation and was allotted the abandoned Druse village of Jermak on Mt. Meiron. There Rabbi Bak and his sons built houses, planted gardens, ploughed, and sowed fields. In her diary entry of 23 May 1839, Lady Judith Montefiore describes her and her husband's visit to Rabbi Bak's settlement. The two Scottish missionaries, Bonar and McCheyne, write of their visit later in the same year, when they found some fifteen settlers, female workers, and farm animals. But the Bak farmstead did not outlast Ibrahim Pasha's defeat and the settlers dispersed.

Bonar and McCheyne also report seeing Jewish agricultural workers at Peqi'in, while other travellers tell of Jewish peasants at Shefar'am, Kafr Yasif, and in several settlements in the Lebanon. The British vice-consul in Akko, Finzi, noted that the Jews of Shefar'am and Kafr Yasif were farmers and paid taxes in wheat and barley. But the real awakening to the idea of Jewish agricultural settlement came with Montefiore's visit. Various plans were submitted to him. Mordekhai Tzoref, a well-known Jerusalem Jew, suggested establishing a settlement in the South, while some of the Jews of Safed and Jerusalem pressed their own preferences. Specific and detailed plans for farming villages near Safed and Tiberias were prepared and there was a proposal for a settlement for people from Jerusalem and Ramla.

Encouraged by this enthusiasm, Montefiore drew up a scheme for leasing two hundred villages in Galilee for settlement by Jewish farmers. His plan even included the establishment of a bank with a capital of £1,000,000 to finance the project. Before submitting the plan to Mohammed Ali he discussed it with the British consul in Jerusalem, who, while advising caution, nevertheless agreed that a move to agriculture would improve the position of the Jews. Mohammed Ali, suspecting that the plan might lead to some sort of independence for the Jews, procrastinated while hinting

103

that it did not seem feasible. Events decided the matter: the Egyptians were forced to leave and negotiations ended. Montefiore pursued his efforts on behalf of the Jews of Palestine in other ways.

Menachem Mendel of **Kamenetz**, a Russian Jew, emigrated to Palestine in 1833 and also settled in Safed. Between 1838 and 1842 he was in Europe soliciting funds for the Jewish community and on his return opened a hotel in Jerusalem to serve as a hostel for new immigrants. In his little book *Korot ha'Etim* (Events of the Time), published in Vilna in 1840, he describes the sufferings of the Jews of Safed resulting from the fellaheen revolt and the earthquake. He also devotes a chapter to the everyday life of the Jews — their occupations, food, household utensils, and even methods of cooking.

Rabbi Joseph **Schwarz**, too, came in 1833 during the Egyptian occupation to live in Palestine. In the preface to his book *Tebu'ot Ha'Aretz* he complains that the Jews of Palestine show no interest in the exploration of their own land and set himself to remedy the situation. The book, first published in 1845, contains much interesting information. He also wrote many letters discussing the history of Palestine and the events of his own time.

A few years later Ritter claimed that most of the current books on Palestine geography were faulty in that they drew too much on references to the Bible and neglected data of their own day and their own observations, thus making unfounded assumptions and unwarranted inferences. Ritter finds Rabbi Joseph Schwarz's approach more acceptable, his work being based on personal on-the-spot observations and investigations. *Tebu'ot ha'Aretz* was translated from Hebrew into German, and in 1850 it appeared in America as *A Descriptive Geography and Brief Historical Sketch of Palestine*. The book is a continuation of Schwarz's earlier book *Tebu'ot ha Shemesh*, on astronomy. Schwarz's work is significant in that it became the basis and model for all subsequent Hebrew writing on Palestine exploration taking Jewish sources into account. Rabbi Schwarz may justifiably be considered the first Hebrew geographer of modern times.

*The Old German (Ashkenazi) synagogue in the Old City of Jerusalem. (Schwarz, 1850, p. 277).*

The English translation of Schwarz's book *"Tebu'oth ha-Aretz"*, published in America, contains a number of illustrations made, on the basis of his data, by a Jewish lithographer named Schuster. The maps were drawn by someone else under Schwarz's personal supervision. A German translation was published in 1852 in Frankfurt-on-Main. Though the illustrations are clear and attractive, they are hopelessly inaccurate and it is impossible to identify the synagogue in the picture.

*Boundary of Palestine. (Schwarz, 1850, p. 32).*

One of the most interesting maps of Palestine, from a Jewish point of view, is that of Rabbi Joseph Schwarz published in Hebrew and English in 1829 before he settled in Jerusalem, and again in 1831 and 1833. The map was again reprinted in the English edition of Schwarz's work *"Tebu'oth ha-Aretz"* in 1850.

106

*Rabbi Joseph Schwarz. (Schwarz, 1850. Frontispiece).*

Schwarz's decision to settle in the Holy Land did not come to him by sudden inspiration. Not satisfied merely to pray and yearn for the Land of Israel, he thoroughly studied all the available literature on the subject. But finding it impossible to uncover the secrets of the country from afar, he settled in Jerusalem in 1833 where, supported by an allowance from abroad, he devoted himself to exploring Palestine. Rabbi Schwarz traversed the length and breadth of the country, gathering information from local people and making his own observations with a learned and critical eye.

107

*The Sephardic Jewish synagogue in Jerusalem. (Carne, 1838, III, p. 92).*

In the mid-thirties, the Jews of Jerusalem successfully appealed to Ibrahim Pasha for permission to restore their dilapidated synagogues in the Old City. One traveller tells us of a synagogue built of stone with a dome in the centre of its wooden roof. Although the building could hold many people it was built in a relatively low place for fear of angering the authorities. The description seems to fit the Sephardic synagogue repaired in 1834. This picture did not give the name of the synagogue. There is some ground for believing that the illustration depicts the Sephardic synagogue immediately after its completion, at the time of an inauguration ceremony.

108

# CHAPTER THREE

# RETURN OF TURKISH RULE (1840-1856)
# THE ENTIRE COUNTRY REDISCOVERED

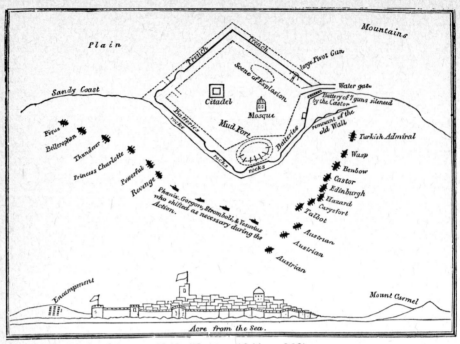

*Plan of the Battle of Acre — 1840. (Hunter, 1841, p. 262).*

On 3 November 1840, a fleet of 21 warships (17 English, the others Austrian and Turkish) arrived off Acre. The allies prepared for a protracted siege since the town was known to be garrisoned by 6,000 men with 150 pieces of artillery in fortified positions, besides field guns. The ships's guns fired explosive shells, very different from the ordinary, solid cannonballs of those days. An ammunition dump was hit, the explosions destroying a large part of the fortifications. In the confusion an Austrian unit penetrated the town and took up positions in the abandoned central tower of the fortress. The following day Acre surrendered and Ibrahim Pasha's Egyptian troops retreated homewards in disorder.

The sketch-map is from Hunter's book on the expedition to Syria. Apart from describing British military actions, Hunter gives details about various towns and villages in the country, particularly along the coast.

110

# REPRESENTATIVES OF THE EUROPEAN POWERS: CONSULS AND RELIGIOUS COMMUNITIES

Considerable changes were introduced in the Ottoman administration of Palestine after Ibrahim Pasha's forced withdrawal in 1840. There was now far more central control as a result of reforms initiated by Sultans Selim III and Mahmoud II earlier in the century. The unruly corps of Janissaries was replaced by a regular army under government control no longer dependent on local pashas or emirs. Moreover, direct collection of taxes by the government during the nine years of highly centralized Egyptian rule had weakened the power of the feudal governors, so that the Turks could now act with a surer hand than previously. Authority, however, was not imposed immediately for tribes and clans rebelled against the new administration. On the Jerusalem road, for example, the men of Abu Ghosh once again extorted tolls from travellers, and the Muslim population of the entire country was still split into the two rival factions — the "Qays" and the "Yaman" — who, reviving old quarrels, once again launched into mutual aggression. At the same time, the imperial government carried out the Turkification of the higher ranks of the local bureaucracy, thus depriving it of its semi-independent status. Officials were transferred from post to post at short intervals; local governors could no longer impose the death sentence and were made answerable for abusing their authority.

All this was the result of the beginning of the Tanzimat period — the reforms first proclaimed by the sultan in 1839. The Tanzimat reforms, reflecting both internal pressures and Western influence — especially after the European powers helped the Turks against Mohammed Ali — provided for equality of rights for the non-Muslim subjects of the Ottoman Empire, and maintained the special status of foreign consuls and Christian churches in Palestine as granted them towards the end of the Egyptian occupation. The European powers, competing for positions of influence in Jerusalem, appointed consuls and high-ranking clergy to watch over their particular interests. In 1838, Mohammed Ali agreed to the establishment of an English consulate in Jerusalem. Until then, European consular representatives had been confined to the coastal towns of Akko,

Haifa, and Jaffa, and to Ramla, and were usually staffed by local agents, their function being commercial rather than political. Thus, in 1820, a Russian consulate was opened in Jaffa to look after the needs of the Orthodox pilgrims. In Jaffa and Haifa, in the days of Ibrahim Pasha, there were British vice-consuls responsible to the consul-general in Alexandria and when the office was opened in Jerusalem, it was headed by a vice-consul who was later promoted to consul-general.

This step by Britain spurred the other powers to follow suit, and within twenty years, all the principal Western nations, including the United States of America, had permanent consular representation in Jerusalem. The effect on Palestine was profound: a new and alien factor began to make its mark on the country. The consuls gradually strengthened their status vis-a-vis the Ottoman governors, until the consulates virtually became governments in miniature. From their reports it can be seen that they regarded the country as territory mortgaged to them. At the same time, however, their presence hastened the process of modernization. The Christian communities too, grew in importance.

The Turkish authorities were not very happy with their foreign residents and put many difficulties in their way. To build a synagogue or church, special permission was required from the sultan, and without an imperial order, non-Muslims could not visit the Muslim holy places. The minorities therefore, confined themselves to their own quarters where they could live according to their own religion and customs. However, quarrels soon broke out among the different Christian communities. In 1808, fire caused serious damage to the Church of the Holy Sepulchre, and the repairs, financed by contributions from the Christian world at large led to immediate trouble. Although the sultan had given special permission for the work to be carried out, the local Muslims rioted in protest. Rivalry as to who should do the sacred work broke out between the Latins, Greeks, and Armenians, but since the Greeks contributed the greater part of the funds, the rights of supervision went to them, resulting in the enhanced status to the Orthodox church. But this did not last long. A new factor began to appear in the Holy Land — the Protestant churches.

Even before Mohammed Ali's rule, Protestant missionaries from Britain and America had pressed for the right to establish permanent institutions in Jerusalem and elsewhere in Palestine, but met with opposition from the provinical governors and their local representatives. Ibrahim Pasha, however, allowed them not only to preach openly but also permitted

112

them to set up schools and other educational institutions. This enabled American, British, and Prussian Protestant clergy to engage in missionary activities among the local population. However, since the law prohibited the conversion of Muslims, they directed their efforts to the local Christian communities and to the Jews. Thus the members of the first Protestant communities in Palestine were drawn from the Greek Orthodox church and included a few proselytized Jews.

The Protestants continued their missionary activities also after the return of the Turks. In 1841, the Anglican and the Prussian Lutheran churches established a joint bishopric headed by a converted Jew, Michael Solomon Alexander. After his death in 1845, Alexander's place was taken by a Swiss missionary, Samuel Gobat. But Protestant missionary endeavours laboured under a handicap compared with the activities of Catholic France and Orthodox Russia, for Protestants had no local Christian communities to base themselves on. England therefore took advantage of the war between Turkey and Mohammed Ali to make herself the self-appointed protector of Palestine's Jewish and Druse communities, while France, not to be outdone, strengthened its existing ties with the Maronites of Lebanon. Other Christian churches too, launched into extensive missionary activities. In 1845, a new Orthodox patriarch was elected to Jerusalem, and a year later, a Russian archimandrite arrived. Russia worked untiringly to increase her influence among the various sections of the Eastern church, and under the terms of the Kuchuk-Kainarji treaty of 1774, claimed the right of protection over the Arabs of the Greek Orthodox faith and of extending its aegis over the Greek Orthodox patriarchate in Jerusalem. The czarist government, with the aid of the Russian Church Mission in the country, and later of the Russian Orthodox community in Palestine, provided funds for the establishment and maintenance of churches, schools, and hostels.

France opened a consulate in Jerusalem in 1843, and now claimed protective rights over the Roman Catholic community, institutions, and the holy places. In 1847, the French restored the Latin monastery on Mount Carmel and persuaded Pope Pius IX to re-establish the Latin patriarchate of Jerusalem abolished shortly after the expulsion of the Crusaders by Salah ed-Din — a move strongly resented by the Franciscans, until then the sole representatives of the Latin West in the Holy Land. The new patriarch promptly set himself to diminish the influence of Orthodox and Protestants alike.

113

*Pool of Siloam. (Bartlett, in Stebbing, 1847, II, p. 146).*

Nineteenth century travellers describe the Pool of Siloam as a small reservoir filled with water by an underground channel from the Gihon spring. From the pool a small rock-hewn conduit carried the water to the fig and other fruit trees planted on the terraces along the slope to the bottom of the Jehoshaphat valley. Some authors thought that an additional underground water conduit brought water from the city itself to the pool. At the confluence of the Jehoshaphat and Hinnom valleys was another water source, the Well of Job (or Joab) — also known as Nehemiah's well — the Biblical Ein Rogel.

The text draws the attention of the beholder to the people at the right descending to the pool, while to the left are women fetching water in jars.

114

*Mount Zion, Jerusalem. (The Nebi Da'ud Mosque). (Horne 1836, I, plate 14).*

The artist, Bulmer, based this picture on a sketch made on the spot by Catherwood. "At the heart of Mt. Zion", the explanation reads, "there is a Turkish mosque called "Nebi Da'ud", built of large black stones. Part of the building contains the Church of the Last Supper — the Coenaculum, while in the mosque itself is shown the tomb of Nebi Da'ud, to gain entrance to which was particularly difficult". "Part of Mt. Zion", continues the author, "is planted with barley and part is ploughed; the soil is mixed with stones and plaster, evidence of past destruction".

Other sources relate that at the beginning of the 19th century only one large building stood on Mt. Zion — the irregularly shaped mosque of Nebi Da'ud. A number of Arab dwellings clung to its outer walls, while between the mosque and the Zion Gate stood a dilapidated building — the Armenian House of Caiphas church. On Mount Zion were a number of cemeteries — Christian: Armenian, Greek and Latin, American and English — as well as Jewish and Muslim.

115

*Entrance to the Church of the Holy Sepulchre. (Carne, 1838, III, p. 79).*

The painter, Allom, who drew this picture, visited the country in 1837 and worked together with Carne and Bartlett in preparing the third volume of *Syria, the Holy Land, Asia Minor etc*. The accompanying explanation relates that, up to the time of Ibrahim Pasha, the key to the church was kept in the citadel by the city governor who requested payments for visiting the church. Ibrahim Pasha changed this practice: visitors now bestowed a gift, according to their inclinations, to the man who fetched the key for them and who waited patiently outside.

On entering the church, one faced the "Stone of Anointing" (shown in the picture) on which, according to Christian tradition, the body of Jesus was laid after being taken from the Cross.

116

Later, France was officially recognized "protector" of the Roman Catholic church in Palestine under article 62 of the Berlin Agreement of 1878, despite the strong opposition of other Catholic countries.

Thus from the end of the thirties of the 19th century, Palestine was subjected to a burst of Christian religious activity. Missionary literature and publications of all kinds expounding messianic messages recalled Biblical prophecies and urged lost souls to join the Christian host. There was hardly a Christian sect not represented by some institution in the country. At the close of the century Jerusalem had the largest missionary concentration in the world, in relation to its population.

To better propagate their particular concepts of Christianity, various Protestant churches and religious groups established a plethora of educational, medical, and charitable institutions. Judging the success of these ventures by the number of converts they attracted, the verdict must be failure, but there can be no doubt that the social effects of the establishment of schools and clinics by Protestant missionaries played a significant part in awakening the country from its stagnation. The challenge they constituted to the Latin and Greek Orthodox churches led these to set up similar institutions of their own. Then, the Turkish authorities, jealous of the successes of foreigners, followed suit in an attempt to compete with the services offered by the Christians. The Jews did the same in order to draw needy co-religionists away from attractions, offered by the Christians, that posed a threat to the community's spiritual and physical existence.

The missionaries, in turn, were exploited by the European powers for their own political ends of extending their influence in the Ottoman Empire. Conversely, the conflict of interests between the Western powers fostered hostility among the local Christian communities, adding fuel to the religious fanaticism of the clergy and monks, who at times came to blows and even bloodshed over their respective rights at the holy places. To the shame of Christendom, such unseemly quarrels usually had to be stopped by Muslim soldiers posted inside the Christian precincts. The result was that any real or imaginery infringement, however small, by one community over the prerogatives of another usually had international political repercussions.

France, Russia, Turkey, and other European powers all became embroiled to such an extent that the dispute over the right to carry out repairs in the

117

Church of the Holy Sepulchre became one of the factors that led to the Crimean War.

The net result of this situation was an increase of direct European influence in the Holy Land.

## PALESTINE: A SELF-CONTAINED GEOGRAPHICAL UNIT. SUMMARY BOOKS.

From the forties of the 19th century, there was a marked increase in the number of travellers who felt impelled to publish their experiences and views for the enlightenment of others. Many of them strove to emulate the great Robinson and to enrich the growing corpus of knowledge with new facts and observations — but seldom with any measure of success. Röhricht's full but still incomplete bibliography of the geography of Palestine from 333 C.E. to 1878 covers some 3,515 authors. Edward Robinson is number 1,886, or about half-way down the list; that is, the number of known works on the subject produced in the forty years from 1838 to the year 1878 is about the same as in the fifteen centuries before Robinson. This enormous accumulation of material gave rise to surveys and summaries of this literature by men who did not necessarily visit the country themselves.

Such a summary was published by John **Kitto** in 1841: *The Physical Geography and Natural History of the Holy Land*. Since at that time geographical knowledge of the country was still very imperfect, the book contains many errors. Yet Kitto made a number of geographical deductions that still provoke discussion today. For example, he discerned two main factors that determine a country's landscape: natural conditions and human activity. It is a combination of the two, he states, that creates what is termed the cultural landscape. He cites Palestine as an example, noting that it is a land of "concentrated" history; that in no other country — even Greece — is the topography so closely linked with past human events. To him, the Holy Land is unique in that the events which so decisively influenced the fate of mankind took place either on its soil or nearby.

118

*Terrace cultivation. (Kitto, 1841, p. 205).*

As early as the 1830's John Kitto, one of the best-known students of Palestine, had arrived at a number of geographical conclusions that are still accepted. In one of his works he describes the seasonal crop changes. "Illustration to the Physical History" is how Kitto describes his pictures of plants, animals, agricultural implements, etc. Although many of his drawings are imaginary and far from the real thing, they help visualize the various concepts. In the above picture, for example, the mountain topography is very exaggerated, but the method of terrace cultivation is well conveyed.

119

Another of Kitto's shrewd observations is that Palestine is *an independent geographical entity*. He explains that "Palestine does not, like most other small countries, constantly remind you that it is physically but part of a large country, from which it is but conventionally separated; but it is a complete country — a compact, distinct, and well-proportioned territory. It offers, as it were, an epitome of all the physical features by which different countries are distinguished, and which very few possess in combination." Most contemporary explorers of Palestine, and many geographers who relied on the accounts of the travellers considered Palestine as the southern part of Syria. Kitto, on the other hand, held that the country is composed of a number of natural regional units, each of distinctive character. This replaced the previously accepted view that the regional divisions were determined only by political and administrative factors. Following Kitto's thesis, explorers now set themselves to determine the natural boundaries of Palestine according to these criteria — mainly of geological formation and climate. Kitto himself defined the borders as follows: the Mediterranean on the west; the southern slopes of Lebanon and the Litani River to the north; the desert line to the south; Wadi El Arish (thought to be Nahal Mitzraim — the "River of Egypt" — of the Bible) the south-west border; and the River Jordan, the Dead Sea and the Arava Valley on the east.

Kitto spent long years studying and teaching the Bible. The first chapter of his book appraises his sources, the most useful according to him being the works of Paxton, Madox, Monro, Hogg, and Elliot. He also mentions Clarke, Burckhardt, Buckingham, Seetzen, Irby and Mangles, Richardson, Madden, George Robinson, Stephens, Lindsay and Skinner. Kitto apparently did not get to see Edward Robinson's *Biblical Researches* for he makes no mention of it. The rest of Kitto's work deals mainly with the physical geography and natural history of Palestine. Numerous inaccuracies and errors leave the impression that Kitto had no first-hand acquaintance with the country and that his book is merely a summary of others. Nevertheless, compared with his contemporaries, the originality of his approach lends his work considerable importance.

In 1844 Kitto brought out *The Pictorial History of Palestine and the Holy Land, including a complete History of the Jews*. Another work — for school children — using material from his first two books is *Palestine, an account of its Geography and Natural History and the customs and institutions of the Hebrews*. It also deals with ancient agriculture and

120

implements, and gives an historical account of Palestine from ancient times to the Crusades. He also published a Biblical atlas in 1850 (second edition: 1873), with maps, topographical sketches, drawings, and explanatory texts, — mostly relating to the areas settled by the twelve tribes.

Works similar to Kitto's are those by Alexander **Keith** and J.F. **Bannister**. In his *Land of Israel according to the Covenant with Abraham, Isaac and Jacob*, which appeared in 1843, Keith relates that at first he only intended writing on Jews and Judaism, but after visiting the Holy Land decided to devote himself to the study of the country promised to the Patriarchs. Bannister's work is mainly an historical and geographical survey. The chapter headings reflect the geographical conception of the time: a) the country's names; the borders; partition of the country by Joshua, David and Solomon, the Romans, and political partition under Turkish rule; b) physical geography — mainly a climatic description; c) mountains, valleys, and plains; d) rivers, lakes, and springs; e) natural history: fertility of the soil, animals, plants etc.; f) cities of Palestine — with a considerable section on Jerusalem.

Four other summary works dealing with the Holy Land, Judaism, and religion are *The Modern Judea compared with ancient prophecy* by James **Wylie**; *The Holy Land: being sketches of the Jews and the Land of Palestine* by the missionary Andrew **Bonar**; *Syria and the Holy Land* by W.K. **Kelly**; and *Palestine* by the French-Jewish intellectual, S. **Munk**.

# EXPLORING THE COURSE OF THE JORDAN AND MAPPING THE INLAND LAKES

Once again military men helped to further the geographical study of Palestine. The British expedition that defeated Ibrahim Pasha in 1840 was accompanied by a survey team headed by Major R.R. Scott. The group made an accurate map of the Syrian and Palestine coast in 1841, using the theodolite as the main instrument for the first time in the region. Lieutenant J.F.A. Symonds, a leading member of the team, carried out surveys between Jaffa and Jerusalem, Jerusalem — the Dead Sea, and along the line Ras el Abiad — Safed — Lake Kinneret. The results of the survey, to a scale of 1:253,440, were not made generally

*Views. Tiberias and Haifa. (Alderson, 1843).*

The British Admiralty survey of the Palestine coast began in 1839 and was concluded after Ibrahim Pasha retreated. The first progress report, published in the journal of the Royal Engineers in 1843, gave many details about Acre, Haifa, Gaza, el-Arish and other towns, as well as maps, illustrations, and sketches. The views of Tiberias and the Carmel are from this publication.

122

available at first, bringing forth complaints from other British explorers. But later, most of the data was released and proved a most reliable source of information in the compilation of new maps.

**R.C. Alderson**, who also participated in the Royal Engineers survey, published part of the findings, in 1844, in his *Notes on Acre*. The book contains maps and drawings of Akko, Haifa, Jaffa, Gaza, El Arish, as well as Tiberias and other coastal towns. Alderson dwells on the state of their fortifications and their general condition in 1841 and gives a brief historical sketch of Akko up to the siege by Napoleon and the battles fought over the town in 1799, in 1831-2 by Ibrahim Pasha, and the bombardment of 1840. There is also an interesting chapter on the streams flowing into the Mediterranean — including also Wadi El-Arish in North Sinai.

At the same time, others including Ludwig von **Wildenbruch** and A.J. **Letronne**, were at work, the former, from 1842 to 1846, making climatological studies and surveying between Jaffa, Jerusalem and the Dead Sea, Jerusalem — Lake Kinneret — the sources of the Jordan, and Beirut to Damascus. Already in 1839, Letronne attempted to determine the difference between the levels of the Dead Sea and the Red Sea, in connection with the projected Suez canal venture. Others tried to determine the water levels of the Gulfs of Suez and Aqaba after Napoleon's engineers had erred in estimating a tidal difference of ten metres between the Red Sea and the Mediterranean.

Strangely, the results of research in the mid-forties were not reflected in the cartography of the period. For example, J. **Van de Cotte** published a series of topographical maps in Brussels, in 1847, that gave no new details whatsoever. Ritter states that they did not improve on the by now largely outdated maps of Jacotin and Berghaus, and had not benefited from the newer material of Robinson, Kiepert, and others. "A very attractive work, but," he says "it appeals to the very early cartographical efforts... produced in the middle ages...serving up the whole legendary medley". Thus despite new data, there was little progress in mapmaking until the Dutch cartographer C.W.M. Van de Velde produced his map of Palestine in 1851 — the best in his day.

In 1847, the Jordan Rift Valley and the Dead Sea were brought to notice once again by the explorations of Lieutenant **Molyneux** of the Royal Navy, who, however, suffered a fate similar to that of Costigan. After

123

making soundings in Lake Kinneret he surveyed the Jordan down to the Dead Sea. Six months after completing his work he died of fever, but unlike Costigan, left a short account of his investigations and a sketch of the Kinneret in a report published in the *Journal of the Royal Geographical Society*, in 1848. Molyneux was the first to determine that the depth of Lake Kinneret does not exceed 48 metres. The same journal contains two other articles on Palestine: "On the Fall of the Jordan" by August Petermann, dealing with the history of exploration and survey of the Jordan Rift Valley. The second is an article by Edward Robinson entitled "Depression of the Dead Sea and of the Jordan Valley".

Important explorations of the Holy Land were undertaken in 1847-48 by the United States Navy under the command of Lieutenant William F. Lynch. Scientifically, the region of the Jordan valley was completely unknown until the beginning of the nineteenth century. Maps of the Jordan, the Dead Sea, and Lake Kinneret were merely sketches lacking precision and detail, and the flora, fauna, and other geographical components of the area had not been studied. Although many travellers had visited the region before Lynch, no one had accurately mapped the area in its entirety.

Lieutenant Lynch began preparations for his voyage by asking the United States government to authorize a naval expedition to the Dead Sea and the River Jordan. In November, with a party that included Lieutenant John B. Dale, Midshipman Richmond Aulick, Francis E. Lynch (the commander's son) and ten seamen, he sailed from Brooklyn, New York, aboard the *Supply*, which was taking provisions to the American squadron in the Mediterranean.

After a journey of three months they landed at Constantinople where the American minister introduced Lynch to the sultan of Turkey. As a result of the audience, Lynch was given a firman permitting exploration in Ottoman territory and ordering the governors of Sidon and Jerusalem to assist the expedition. From Constantinople they travelled along the coast to Beirut and to Akko where Lynch disembarked with his party. The ship was to proceed with its normal duties in the Mediterranean and later return for the expedition at Beirut.

From Akko, Lynch and his party started on the overland journey to Tiberias and Lake Kinneret with two specially made metal boats — the copper *Fanny Mason* and the iron *Fanny Skinner* — on two low trucks.

124

*Akil Aga. (Lynch, 1849, p. 128).*

By descent and character Akil Aga was a Bedouin. At the time of the Lynch expedition he headed the Bani Huwara tribe which had migrated from Egypt during Jazzar
Pasha's rule in Acre. At the end of the 18th century, the Bani Huwara joined the
rebels, but with the return of the Turks they gave strong support to the new regime
in Acre. Akil Aga forged friendly ties with the other Bedouin tribes and was able to
pacify the turbulent Banu Sakhr. He was known for his friendly relations with foreigners, especially with Jews and Christians. The American expedition secured his protection and he served them faithfully, risking his life when men of another tribe attacked
the expedition after it refused to accept their protection. As a result of Lynch's account, Akil Aga became known in Europe and America, and other travellers mentioned
him in their books. This is the only known picture of this colourful personality.

125

*The Lynch caravan. (Lynch, 1849, p. 147).*

A typical scene: the caravan on its way from Acre to Tiberias. The camels laden with stores move slowly, with the guards on watch for robbers who might lie in ambush behind the wild shrubbery. The American flag flies from the boat.
Lynch gives a brief introduction to the beautiful woodcuts in his book and praises Lieutenant Dale who made the sketches but died before he could complete the work.

126

*Ain Jidy. (En Gedi). (Lynch, 1849, p. 290).*

On 2 April 1848, the Lynch expedition anchored near the mouth of the stream of Ain Jidy (Nahal David), but not finding a suitable camping site there they moved 700 metres southwards, where they set up their tents. At the delta they saw signs of cultivation — apparently land abandoned because of tribal disputes. In the evening, representatives of the Ta'amra tribe visited the camp and a feast was prepared in their honour.

127

The caravan must have been an imposing sight — two boats with American flags, on trucks drawn by camels; officers and seamen mounted on horseback, loaded camels, attendants, and Arabian chieftains with their retinues. After five days the expedition reached Lake Kinneret, and with flags flying, the boats were launched upon the blue waters of the lake. The Arabs sang and clapped their hands in rhythm, crying for backsheesh. Because April was the most suitable time for rowing the Jordan, Lynch decided to postpone his survey of Lake Kinneret and immediately descended the river. Part of the expedition travelled by boat, while the remainder went on foot as land guards. Each man was assigned certain duties such as mapping the topography of the river and its shores, observing the water volume in the river and its tributaries, and recording the natural features of the valley. Due to the frequent rapids, especially in the section from the Kinneret to the junction of the Yarmuk River, the journey entailed a succession of dangers and excitement.

After an eight-day sail down the Jordan, the expedition reached the Dead Sea and began the most important part of the mission. The itinerary included a voyage along the coasts starting on the western shore, a survey of the Lashon Peninsula, and finally a journey up the eastern shore. Lynch planned to take frequent soundings by crossing from shore to shore and also scheduled visits to places of interest in the area.

Immediately after entering the Dead Sea a storm developed and the expedition was forced to hug the coast. On the second day they encamped on the western shore opposite Nahal David (Wadi Sudeir), a little below En Gedi, and selected a site for headquarters, which they named Camp Washington. From there they explored the famous Sebbeh-Massada remains. While on the Lashon Peninsula, Lynch named the northern promontory Point Costigan, and the south-western promontory Point Molyneux after the two explorers who preceded him there. Earlier, in Tiberias, when Lynch had heard of their sad fates, he had promised that "If God spares us, we will commemorate their gallantry and their devotion to the cause of science."

Before leaving the area, the expedition journeyed fifteen miles east, to Kerak, a climb of three thousand feet. On 10 May, after surveying for twenty-two days, they completed their exploration in the Dead Sea. As a memorial to their visit, Lynch ordered a float bearing an American flag constructed in the lake.

From the Dead Sea the expedition moved to Jerusalem, passing the monastery of Mar Saba, then to the Mediterranean near Jaffa several days later, and finally returned to Tiberias in June. Lynch planned to explore Lake Kinneret but cancelled the trip when a boat specially designed to replace the other boats, which had been damaged in the Dead Sea exploration, did not arrive on time. Instead, after visiting Lake Hula and the sources of the Jordan, the expedition pushed on to the valley of the Litani, Mount Hermon, Damascus, and Baalbek. Accomplishing this in two weeks proved to be exhausting, especially after the extensive work on the Dead Sea. When at Baalbek, sickness overcame the expedition, Lynch quickly moved to Beirut where he had arranged to meet the *Supply*, but many were down with fever by the time they reached the city. Among those stricken was Lieutenant Dale, who died a few days later from the same nervous fever that had taken the lives of Costigan and Molyneux. Lynch waited for the *Supply* for one month, when, finally growing impatient and fearful of disease in the town, he hired another ship and sailed for Malta. In the meantime, the *Supply* not finding Lynch in Beirut, returned to Malta and rejoined the expedition. On September 12, Lynch and his party sailed for the United States.

Upon his return Lynch published two books about his travels: *The Narrative of the United States' Expedition to the River Jordan and the Dead Sea* and the *Official Report of the United States' Expedition to Explore the Dead Sea and the River Jordan*. The former was written hurriedly because Lynch learned that another member of the expedition was about to publish his own account of the journey. In the preface to the book Lynch discusses the purpose of the expedition and justifies its expense to the American people who, he hoped, "would not long condemn an attempt to explore a distant river, and its wondrous reservoir, — the first, teeming with sacred associations, and the last, enveloped in a mystery, which had defied all previous attempts to penetrate it." In the first part of the book he lists the names and functions of each member of the party, the preparations for the voyage and the Atlantic crossing, and a detailed account of the exploration in the Holy Land including thirty woodcuts depicting the people and events of the trip. The second book, the *Official Report*, was very different from the *Narrative*, which contained material he believed unsuitable for a public document. The *Official Report* consists of governmental documents concerning the expedition, minutes taken during the descent of the Jordan and the Dead Sea, reports by members of the expedition on the bird and plant life, and the geology of the region. In addition, the book contains astronomical, thermometric, and barometric tables, an analysis of Dead Sea water, a table of meteorological observations, a map of the route and camps of the expedition, and sketch maps of the Jordan and the Dead Sea. Unlike the *Narrative*, it does not include drawings of the landscape.

Scholars eagerly awaited the publication of his books, and the *Narrative* with its maps and drawings was rapidly published in many different editions. Lynch was regarded as an explorer who had braved much, persevered, and accomplished work of great significance to science. In the *Official Report* he himself writes with optimism and pride:

> The exploration of this (the Dead Sea) was now complete; we had carefully sounded its depths, determined its geographical position, taken topographical sketches of its shores, ascertained the temperature, width, depth, velocity of its tributaries, collected specimens of its own and of its tributary waters and of every kind of mineral, plant, and flower, and noted the winds, currents, changes of weather and all atmospheric phenomena. These with a succinct account of events exactly as they transpired will give a correct idea of this sea as it has appeared to us. The same remark holds with respect to the Jordan and the country through which it flows.

Although Lynch certainly overestimated his accomplishments in the Dead Sea, which even today has not been fully investigated, his achievements on the whole were enormous. He was the first to make an accurate and detailed map of the Jordan and the Dead Sea. He confirmed the level of the Dead Sea and drew an accurate bathymetric map. The *Official Report* and the *Narrative* also provide information about historical relics no longer extant. A devout Christian, Lynch regarded the Jordan and surrounding country as sacred and paid strict attention to remnants of bridges, khans, milestones, caves, buildings, ancient agricultural cultivation, wells, and cisterns. Lynch's works, especially the *Narrative*, give a vivid picture of the cultural landscape of the region in the mid-nineteenth century, which was the beginning of the modern age in Palestine. Events in Palestine since the expedition, especially those of the twentieth century, have destroyed many of these sites, and Lynch's studies, as well as those of other nineteenth-century explorers, provide valuable details in reconstructing many of these monuments.

It did not take long for these spectacular discoveries to be reflected in the Palestine travel literature of the time. J.A. **Spencer**, an Episcopalian clergyman and theologian, who toured the country in 1849, already

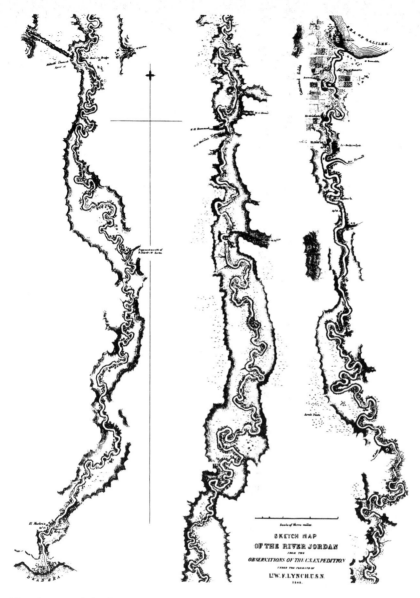

*Sketch map of the Jordan. (Lynch, 1849, p. 13).*

Although rough and very inaccurate, this map was the first to show the course of the river and enables us to compare it with modern maps. The Jordan is known for its meanders that change their course within short periods of time. The expedition's progress was hazardous, particularly near the confluence of the Yarmuk. Of its three boats — two of metal and one of wood — the last was damaged and sank.

131

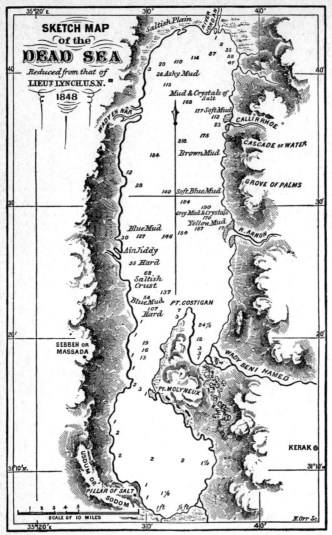

*Sketch-map of the Dead Sea, reduced from that of Lynch.*
*(Spencer, 1850, p. 385).*

The Lynch expedition to the Dead Sea and the results of his soundings were of great scientific value. The 166 soundings were carried out in five west-to-east lines connected to one another by a diagonal. The maximum depth of the sea was found to be approximately 400 metres. The map also includes data of the shore and the surrounding area. The steep gradients of the mountain slopes descending to the Dead Sea shore are indicated by hachures. The value of the map was quickly recognized by other explorers, who made much use of it.

132

included a copy of Lynch's map of the Jordan Valley in his book. Although disclaiming any scientific value for his work, Spencer provides useful material on the country and the way of life of its inhabitants.

Capitan William **Allen**, R.N., who travelled the country in 1850, wrote *The Dead Sea, New Route to India* which was published in 1855, and also gives details about the Jordan Rift Valley and the Dead Sea and some explanations of their formation. One chapter deals with the destruction of Palestine's forests. Allen includes Molyneux's sketch and measurements of the Kinneret. Another author worth mentioning is the Prussian preacher H. **Gadow**, who wrote two accounts of his travels that took him to Jericho and Mar Saba.

# JERUSALEM: NEW DIMENSIONS OF RESEARCH

Edward Robinson's *Biblical Researches* gave rise to sharp controversy concerning the topography of Jerusalem and the location of the holy sites. Opinions were split chiefly on the authenticity of the site of the Holy Sepulchre. The problem, unresolved to this day, hinges on the exact course of the second wall of Jerusalem at the time of the Crucifixion. The present, traditional site of the Holy Sepulchre might be genuine only if it can be proven to be outside the line of the second wall, for Jews could not be buried within the city. The known literary sources being vague on this subject, every concerned traveller sought archaeological evidence to solve this vital problem.

Robinson and other Protestant investigators considered the traditionally hallowed site as improbable, if not impossible. The question was therefore laden with sectarian and even political implications. Devout Catholics were scandalized by such scepticism, but the traditional view was also forcefully upheld by George **Williams**, a former chaplain to the Anglican Bishop Alexander. Williams's book, which is of great value, also gives a wealth of information on Jerusalem in the mid-nineteenth century, and contains a plan of the city based on surveys made in 1841 by a team of Royal Engineers under Lieuts. Alderson and Aldrich. Another book about the city propounding the traditionalist argument, W. **Krafft**'s *Die Topographie Jerusalems*, earned praise from Ritter. But the most important explorer of the Holy City in the forties was Titus **Tobler**, who visited Palestine

*Street in Jerusalem. (Lady Tennison, 1846, plate 16).*

Houses about to collapse and foul streets, crowded living conditions, a lack of the most elementary facilities — these are subjects travellers wrote about to describe the desolation of the Holy City and the backwardness of its inhabitants. At the same time artists captured the architectural beauty of buildings, the lengthening perspective, the corner of a shadowy street, the play of light and shade in the twisting alleyways, the tones of colour in the chiselled stone walls, or the slippery steps of the streets. This picture from Lady Tennison's album is typical of such romantic impressions.

134

*The Gihon (Siloam) Spring. (Piscine de Siloé à Jerusalem).*
*(Munk 1841, plate 25).*

Munk's book on Palestine is one of the most important general books on the Holy
Land of the forties. It was first published in 1845 and contains sketches of sites and of
implements, household equipment, dress, etc. Some of the illustrations are taken from
earlier sources. The above view is an example of one of these.

135

*Valley of Jehoshaphat, Jerusalem. (Horne, 1836, I, p. 83;*
*Olin, 1843, II, p. 142).*

The Kidron valley with its monuments from the time of the Second Temple was part of Jerusalem's Jewish cemetery in the 19th century. It was considered a great privilege for Jews from both Palestine and the Diaspora to be buried there, particularly near the Tomb of Zachariah. It is interesting to note that, at that time, the name Kidron was used by the Jews and Christians but not by the Muslims. Close by the impressive ancient monuments numerous tombstones can be seen, while to the left, part of the bridge over the Kidron valley is visible (See also p. 18). The illustration is from Olin who reproduced it from Horne. The artist is Roberts, who drew the picture before his visit to Palestine and without having seen the site.

136

*Bird's-eye view of Jerusalem from the south. Said to be taken at sunrise.
(Williams, 1849, II, p. 600).*

Jerusalem was closest to the hearts of the travellers, and was, of all the places in the
Holy Land, the most frequently described and depicted. Aware of the interrelation of
geography and historical development, they studied the city's topography in search of
Jerusalem's past.

This sketch has the appearance of an aerial photograph; having most probably been
drawn from a height to the south. The shadows and light give a sense of height and
depth, and despite many inaccuracies, the city's topography is well-presented.

Williams, one of the most important 19th century explorers of Jerusalem, includes
this picture, made on the basis of the survey of Jerusalem by the Royal Engineers in
his book. This survey map was made early in the 1840's when the entire city was
concentrated within the walls, with only a few sites, such as David's Tomb on Mt.
Zion, the Absalom monument, and the Church of the Ascension on the Mount of
Olives outside the city area.

Inside the city walls can be distinguished the Temple compound (Haram) with the
Dome of the Rock and the el-Aqsa mosque, and the Birket Isra'il pool north of it, the
Armenian cathedral church, the citadel, and the Church of the Holy Sepulchre. There
are considerable empty spaces in the Armenian and Jewish quarters, inside the eastern
wall, around the Muristan, and inside the north-western and north-eastern angles of
the wall.

137

*Jews' place of wailing. (The Western Wall).*
*(Bartlett, 1844, p. 141; Stebbing, 1847, II, p. 145).*

"In the shadow of the wall, on the right, were seated many venerable men, reading the book of the law ... There were also many women in their long white robes, who as they entered the small area, walked along the sacred wall, kissing its ancient masonry, and praying through the crevices with every appearance of deep devotion;" Thus Bartlett describes the scene on which he based one of his best known pictures. He writes that he heard no wailing nor saw any "outward signs of sorrow; the scene is sufficiently expressive without such manifestations."

138

again a second time in the following decade to complete the work of his first journey. Tobler set himself the formidable task of making a comprehensive survey of Jerusalem and its surroundings. Among his numerous works, one of the most important is *Topographie von Jerusalem u. Seinen Umgebungen*, published in two parts in Berlin, in 1853 and 1854. The topography of the city, the walls, gates, principal buildings, churches, mosques and synagogues are described in the first part. Tobler accepts Edward Robinson's opinion that Jesus could not have been buried where the Church of the Holy Sepulchre now stands, but that the place should be sought outside the modern city walls. The book contains numerous illustrations and a plan of Jerusalem drawn according to his instructions from on-the-spot sketches. The second part of the book is devoted to the city's surroundings and the areas between Jaffa and the Jordan and between Solomon's Pools and Ramallah. About seventy places are described and, like Robinson before him, Tobler provides the historical background of each site. Tobler also wrote many important monographs, among them on Bethlehem, the Siloam "Spring", and the Mount of Olives, and on Golgotha, its churches and monasteries. He also published a survey of Jerusalem's medical topography, and a diary, *Denkblätter aus Jerusalem*. Two further trips, in 1857 and 1865, resulted in additional monographs — as discussed below.

Three consuls, Ernst Gustav Schulz, K. Basili, and James Finn who represented Germany, Russia, and Britain respectively, published memoirs on their period of service in Palestine. Their extended residence in the region enabled them to gather a store of experiences and to acquire first-hand understanding of the people and the country. Their writings about Jerusalem are more authoritative and far richer in information than those by ordinary visitors.

**Schulz**, the German consul, was an extreme traditionalist regarding the holy sites in Jerusalem. He also wrote an account of six tours in Galilee and Samaria — areas not well-known in his day.

**Basili's** area of jurisdiction covered Syria, his Palestine headquarters being in Beirut. The fifteen years (1839—1853) he spent there, were, he tells his readers, the best of his life. His book written between 1846 and 1847 was published in Odessa in 1862. (James Finn, one of the leading personalities of his day in Jerusalem, will be dealt with separately, below).

Among the very many travellers of those years who have left us accounts are the woman globe trotter, Ida **Pfeiffer** of Vienna, Major D. **Millard**, and the Viscount **Castlereagh**, a member of Parliament who visited Palestine in 1845. The pastor George **Fisk** who speaks of the ever-mounting interest in everything occurring in the Holy Land, discusses what he sees as the impending revival of Palestine and a resurgence of the Jewish people in the pure spirit of Christianity.

A number of Jews who converted to Christianity wrote from their particular point of view, evincing great interest in the inhabitants of the Land of Israel. Ridley **Herschell** felt impelled, like many converts, to convey his new faith to his former co-religionists and engaged in missionary labours. He entitled his book, *A visit to my Father-land...*

Spiritual need led the convert W.J. **Woodcock** to the Holy Land and to publish his travel diary for the benefit of his friends. Modestly he explains that it is difficult to add to what has been written by previous visitors and that he leaves the description of the condition of the Jews to his fellow-traveller and fellow-convert Moses **Margoliouth**, who published *A Pilgrimage to the Land of my Fathers* in 1850.

It is hardly worthwhile to enumerate the travellers of those years. About 300 books and articles were recorded by Röhricht, most of the accounts being repetitive and tedious. Among those travellers who contributed some new geographical information was the American Sam **Wolcott**, a careful observer whose notes of Syria and Palestine were published in the periodical *Bibliotheca Sacra* in 1843. One report has a sketch of the western shore of the Dead Sea, following his visit to Massada. The same journal contains Major F.H. Robe's notes on the area around the Jordan sources. Other issues of *Bibliotheca Sacra* of 1843–1844, give several reports by Eli Smith, Robinson's companion in Palestine in 1838, including notes on Bet Guvrin, Megiddo, Ram (Rama), Jaba' (Geva), Rachel's Tomb, and other places. Konstantin **Tischendorf**, better-known for his discovery and acquisition of the famed Sinai codex than for his contribution to the travel literature on Palestine, the Count de **Pardieu**, J.L. **Patterson**, F.A. **Neale**, and L.H. **Dupuis** are a few other authors whose books contain some noteworthy material.

The Scotsman John **Wilson** came to the country from India where he had lived for fifteen years. This gave him an advantage over most European travellers for he knew Arabic and was familiar with Oriental customs. In his book, he describes areas almost never investigated by earlier

140

*David, son of Rabbi Samuel Moshe the Second, Chief Rabbi of Jerusalem. (Woodcock, 1849. Frontispiece).*

The sympathy with which Woodcock made this portrait shows his affection for the Rabbi's son. Woodcock, a converted Jew and a missionary, went to Palestine to preach to the Jews. Although he had abandoned his native religion one senses in his writings a love for his people living in the land of their fathers. Two appendixes in his book are devoted entirely to them: one on missions to the Jews, the other on the different communities. The author tells of a Jewish woman in Hebron spotting him as being a Jew from Poland who had become a Christian only a few months before. He also tells of young Jews constantly questioning him about his origin and seeking to understand his conversion.

141

visitors. For his own map of Palestine, Wilson relied on Kiepert and Ritter and uses Major Robe's measurements as well as those of the British Admiralty engineers and articles in *Bibliotheca Sacra*. The book gives a plan of Jerusalem based on Schulz, a list of major Biblical sites, remarks on Arabic script, and a note on Oriental Jews, the Samaritans, and others. Wilson, who was a fellow of the Royal Society and of the Royal Asian Society, was a learned and judicious observer. His work is one of the more important ones of the period.

A survey of the contributors to the exploration of Palestine must also lead to the painter W.H. **Bartlett**, who, following his initial visit, published the illustrated book, *Walks in and about the City and Environs of Jerusalem*. The first edition in 1844, was so well received that several more were produced.

Bartlett remarks that only when he saw the country's landscape for himself did he realise that what he had previously painted from the descriptions of others could never convey the true appearance of Jerusalem. He expresses the hope that his readers will now enjoy a clear and complete picture of the Holy City. However, he adds that his delineation of the ancient part, based on the wonderful work of Robinson, does not agree with all of the latter's theories. Bartlett assures his readers that he did not embellish his pictures but presented the views and scenery accurately and faithfully. The book contains a map of Jerusalem, a cross-section of the city, and a description of the route from Jaffa.

The illustrations in Henry **Stebbing**'s *The Christian in Palestine or Scenes of Sacred History* are by Bartlett. Stebbing explains his aim to be the portrayal of both the historical character and the present condition of the land.

Bartlett produced two other books after his first visit: *Forty days in the Desert on the Track of the Israelites...* and *Footsteps of Our Lord and His Apostles*. After his second visit in 1853, he wrote *Jerusalem Revisited*, which was published after his death in the Mediterranean, on his voyage home.

The first to depict Massada was the Englishman William **Tipping**, who showed daring in seeking out places far off the beaten track. Many of his drawings were used to illustrate books on Palestine, including a new English edition of Josephus's *The Jewish War*. Another illustrated book is

*Baths and city of Tiberias, (Mount Hermon in the distance).*
*(Bartlett, Stebbing, 1847, p. 81).*

The hot springs were the sole attraction of the town of Tiberias in the 19th century. Ibrahim Pasha built a new bath-house, in place of the previous structure, to serve the many visitors from all over Syria who sought a cure for their ailments. It was built of white stone; a circular marble hall containing a pool was surrounded by rooms. The spring waters were now for the first time conveyed to the bath-house where they were cooled to a suitable temperature. Bartlett tells how he went there by boat from Tiberias, and then ascended a nearby mountain to the lookout-point, from where he made this drawing.

*Encampment at the Tiberias hot springs. (Egerton, 1841, p. 72).*

Lady Egerton showed particular interest in the Jews of Palestine, being convinced that the coming of the Messiah was at hand and that the exiled Jewish people would soon return to their homeland.

144

that by the Dresden landscape painter Otto **Georgi**, *Die heiligen Stätten nach Originalzeichnungen nach der Natur*, but many of the illustrations are by Heinrich von Mayr. *Syrie ancienne et moderne. Histoire et description* by Joanne **Yanoski** and Jules David also has a large number of illustrations of Palestine.

Of the books of a more general character, Elliot **Warburton**'s *The Crescent and the Cross, or Romance and Realities of Eastern Travel* became very popular and was reprinted in many editions.

Famous artists such as Edward Lear and William Holman-Hunt lived many years in Jerusalem making it a subject of their work. Holman-Hunt, true to the principles of the Pre-Raphaelite Brotherhood, went to Jerusalem to find live models for paintings on Biblical subjects. Frustrated in his attempts to get local people to sit for him, he travelled to the salt flats south of the Dead Sea, taking along a goat for a painting of *The Scapegoat* against a background of the mountains of Moab. This became one of his best-known works. Opposite the Mar Elias monastery, on the road to Bethlehem and Hebron, there stands a stone bench erected by his widow in memory of the artist who used to rest at that spot while taking in the panorama of the city and the hills. Holman-Hunt lived in the Street of the Prophets, in one of the first buildings outside the walls of Jerusalem. Edward Lear is less known for his paintings than for his illustrated books of travel. A close friend of Holman-Hunt, he also made fine panoramic paintings of Jerusalem.

The advent of the camera early in the second half of the 19th century did not displace the artist, though now photographs began to appear in books along with reproductions of paintings, lithographs, engravings, and drawings.

# CARL RITTER AND VAN DE VELDE: MID-CENTURY IN RETROSPECT

The fourteen volumes dealing with the Holy Land and the adjacent regions — Sinai, Transjordan, Syria, and the Lebanon — forming part of the *Erdkunde von Asien* by the great German geographer and historian, Carl **Ritter**, were a major contribution to the geographical knowledge of

145

Palestine. Ritter's monumental work is characterised by its scientific approach, surpassing all that preceded it. The author made use of all the previously published literature — the Old and New Testaments, Josephus and Philo of Alexandria, the Talmud, medieval Christian writings, the works of Arab geographers, as well as the accounts of pilgrims and travellers.

Ritter was a master of organization. Each region of the country is dealt with systematically; starting with a Biblical synopsis, and going on to an historical reconstruction, and a detailed description of the regions traversed by the principal communication routes. Taking the Hebron-Jerusalem road, for example, he describes the physical characteristics of the region; the human settlements, their location and approach routes; building methods; utilization of land and agricultural produce, natural vegetation, and much else. There is much emphasis on the main thoroughfares, distances being given in riding hours. Perhaps this detailed treatment of the subject is due to Ritter having been an instructor in a German military academy. The Biblical places of habitation — particularly the large towns — are dealt with in great detail — more so than geological, climatic, biological, and other natural phenomena; research in these fields was still in its incipient stage in Ritter's time and his knowledge of them was not only meagre but sometimes inaccurate. On the other hand, his anthropo-geographical descriptions are authoritative and precise.

Ritter compares the accounts of travellers with Biblical and other ancient descriptions of the same places. Thus, for example, he examines the Biblical passages mentioning the Qishon River in relation to the descriptions of the stream and its surroundings by Edward Robinson. In evaluating the works of travellers and explorers he does not only speak of their accomplishments, but also points to what they failed to see.

Ritter's comprehensive work includes a bibliography of the literature and maps of Palestine published up to his day. His list of maps is one of the most important means for the study of the cartography of Palestine in the first half of the 19th century. In Ritter's view the cartography of the country only reached acceptable standards with Seetzen.

However, Ritter never visited Palestine. His vast achievement must thus be credited to a fine intuitive sense, and a full mastery and detailed knowledge of the literature.

146

If Carl Ritter's literary work constitutes a kind of compendium of Palestine geography, then, cartographically, Karl **Zimmermann**'s atlas of 1850 complements it. The fourth part of the atlas contains maps of Syria and Palestine to a scale of 1:333,333, covering all that scholars knew or believed about the geography of Palestine.

Lieutenant C.W.M. **van de Velde** was a successful cartographer. While in the Dutch colonial service he made a series of maps of Java that are still regarded as among the best examples of the cartography of the first half of the 19th century. His map of Palestine was published in English and French in eight sheets, to a scale of 1:315,000 along with a volume of memoirs to the map-making process and listing his observations. There is also a map of Jerusalem (1:10,000) and its immediate vicinity (1:250,000). Van de Velde made use of Kiepert's maps of 1842 and of de Saulcy's cartographical work of the Dead Sea area, and also incorporated the astronomical findings of Symonds and his colleagues, the measurements of Lynch and Molyneux and information from Robinson's work, among others. Van de Velde carried out his work by the azimuthal projection method and by estimating the road distances along his way. Despite these primitive methods of surveying, his map was the best and most reliable available until 1876 when the Palestine Exploration Fund brought out their *Great Map of Western Palestine*.

Van de Velde repeatedly crossed and recrossed the country in length and breadth in the course of his work. The narrative of these travels, related in letters to a friend, was published in two volumes in 1854 — one of the best route journals of travels in the Holy Land combining shrewd observations with entertaining anecdotes of his personal adventures. Van de Velde visited the country again in 1862 and published a revised edition of his map as well as an album of one hundred handsome lithographs in colour of scenes and landscapes of the Holy Land.

Ritter's writings and van de Velde's map, together may be considered the crowning achievement of fifty years exploration and research in the geography of Palestine.

Thus, by mid-century, the enormous increase of published material on Palestine reflected a change in the approach of travellers and explorers. If at the beginning of the century travellers were driven by the desire to discover and penetrate unknown districts, and to be the first to claim the credit for their contribution to geographical science, now more systematic

147

*El-Muhraka, site of Elijah's sacrifice. (Van de Velde, 1857, plate 48).*

Van de Velde travelled extensively in Palestine while making one of the best maps of the country. In addition to his exhausting field measurements he also found time to sketch interesting places. From Haifa he made excursions to the Carmel and visited el-Muhraka, the traditional place where the prophet Elijah set up his altar. This is Van de Velde's impression of the site.

148

*Le Rocher de Masada, la Mer Morte. (Massada and the Dead Sea).*
*(Van de Velde, 1857, plate 68).*

In this lithograph Massada is shown from an unusual angle. The artist, in chosing his vantage-point has created a play of perspective that gives a feeling of both depth and distance. The original, in colour, is reproduced in Van de Velde's album of 100 views of the Holy Land, *Le Pays d'Israel.*

149

*El-Khalil (Hebron). (Van de Velde, 1857, plate 67).*

At the beginning of the 19th century, Hebron was an unwalled town sprawling across a valley. The governor's residence, the mosque and the Haram enclosure stood on the east side. Remains of gates and of an ancient wall indicate that Hebron was at one time a fully walled city. It received its water from two pools outside the built-up area. At the beginning of the century the town's population was about 5,000, reaching 8,000 at mid-century. The town was surrounded by vineyards, olive groves, and orchards stretching out for some distance. Hebron became known for its glass-making, thought to have been introduced there in the 12th century by Jews from Venice.

Like in most of his illustrations, Van de Velde improves on reality by showing a tidy-looking town in a park-like setting.

150

*Ruines à Ludd (Lydde). (Van de Velde, 1857, plate 57).*

The proximity of Lod to Ramla invites a comparison of the two as competitors. Lod flourished in periods of Christian rule, while Ramla was built in the 8th century as the provincial Muslim capital. As one prospered, the other declined. In the first half of the 19th century, Lod is described as a poor, unimportant town, its small houses built of scattered stones from ancient ruins. Travellers only stopped there to see the ruins of the Crusader church of St. George, the patron saint of England. Van de Velde's view shows the mosque built into the remains of the church.

151

*Le Lac de Tibériade. (The Sea of Galilee). (Van de Velde, 1857, plate 80).*

As in most of the Tiberias illustrations of the last century, the wall, sea, and mountains combine to give the town its picturesque setting. Yet the visitors usually note that the harmonious, pleasing exterior belied the poverty and neglect that characterized the town. Before the 1837 earthquake there was one gate in the wall which extended along the three land sides of the town. But during the catastrophe, much of the wall collapsed and in other parts cracks appeared. It was never repaired, the breaches eventually becoming passageways. It is interesting to note that even within the walls some parts of the town, mainly to the north, were not built and have remained empty.

152

efforts were made to know and understand the country as a whole. The main object of study was still sacred geography, for many of the travellers were learned in the Scriptures. Among them were a good number of Protestant missionaries and clergymen, coming on the wave of economic prosperity in Europe and America, and of the religious revival of the period. These men devoted but little attention to social questions and local issues, and were not greatly concerned with the native populations and their problems. At most, they tried to explain the neglected state of the country by alluding to the condition of its inhabitants.

On the other hand, the local people took little interest in the visitors whose purpose they did not comprehend. Students of geography and Bible, roaming archaeologists, naturalists, or mapmakers appeared strange to people sunk into illiteracy and superstition. Only imperial letters of protection assured the visitors against attack and abuse. In the eyes of the Muslim inhabitants, this was surely a strange phenomenon: strangers — and Christians at that — go about freely through the countryside, while believing Muslims are prohibited, on pain of stringent punishment, to rob or annoy them, are obligated to fulfill their every wish and to serve them, and are reduced to begging for "baksheesh"!

# THE COUNTRY REFLECTS ITS PEOPLE:
# A.P. STANLEY

Edward **Robinson** and his friend Eli Smith returned to Palestine in 1852 to retrace part of their route of fourteen years before. This time Robinson focussed his interest on Galilee, Samaria, Mount Lebanon, and Damascus, places they had not previously visited. Smith accompanied him to Jerusalem and through Samaria to the foot of Mount Hermon, and then set off on his own to Sidon, while the American missionary, Dr. William M. Thomson replaced him at Robinson's side for a visit to Banias, Hatzbaya, and Damascus. Thence they went to Baalbek and Mount Lebanon, ending the tour in Beirut, full of new observations and discoveries.

Considering that his total working time during the two journeys in the country was only five months, Robinson's achievements are truly astounding. His travels added a close network of survey lines to the map of Palestine — mainly for the Judean Mountains and, to a lesser extent, the mountains of Samaria, Galilee, Lebanon, and Syria. The coast from Gaza to Tyre remained blank except for Akko and he did not investigate Ashqelon, Ashdod, Caesarea, the Carmel, Sulam Tzor (the Ladder of Tyre), and other points along the coast. Robinson hardly set foot east of the Jordan except to discover ancient Pella and examine the sources of the Jordan. He was prevented from visiting the Horan, because of the insecure conditions there; illness forced him to relinquish a visit to Homs and Antioch in northern Syria.

Carefully planning his progress, he never retraced a route, except for the short section between Jerusalem and Bethlehem. He never hurried, and reportedly never showed emotion at his discoveries. Robinson's greatest outburst of enthusiasm was his remark that the natural bridge spanning the Litani River gorge was "magnificent". Nevertheless, elation shows through the account of his discovery of the sites of Bet Guvrin and Idna.

Robinson's main interest was in Biblical Palestine, and the study of Biblical geography was therefore the purpose of his first journey. He later extended the scope of his work to cover the physical and historical geography of Palestine and planned a book in two parts, the first dealing with Palestine, Lebanon, and Sinai as the core of the region, and the second part with the neighbouring countries. Each part was to have three sections — physical geography, historical geography, and historical topography. However, he understood the magnitude of the task and knew that it would be left for others to complete. He hoped nevertheless to finish the first part, but, as his widow writes in the introduction of the book that was published posthumously in 1865, "It was otherwise decreed". He wrote only one part, on the "Physical Geography", and even then, the paragraphs on flora and fauna are fragmentary. A chapter, "The Physical Geography of Syria Proper", which appears as an appendix to his book is really the beginning of his planned second work. His second journey had resulted in the *Later Biblical Researches in Palestine and the Adjacent Regions*, published in 1856, which Kiepert used for a revised version of his map of Palestine.

Claude Conder of the Palestine Exploration Fund considered Robinson's work as the basis of all Biblical research, and it is not until George Adam Smith, whose first journey was made after the period covered in these pages, that we find any comparable contribution to the geography of Palestine.

154

The French explorer Félicien de **Saulcy**, member of the Institut Français, made the journey to Palestine in 1850, hoping to explore lesser-known sites, starting with the Dead Sea area. However, he became better known for his excavation of the "Tombs of the Kings" in Jerusalem. On a first visit in 1851, de Saulcy made a preliminary survey of the site and it was only on his return, twelve years later, armed with a firman from the Turkish authorities, that he carried out the dig.

The British clergyman, Dean Arthur P. **Stanley** visited Palestine in 1852, and again in 1862. His popular book, *Sinai and Palestine*, is original in concept and marked by characteristics of its own in its method of description, its structure, and its approach to the geography and history of the country.

Stanley describes Palestine as "an island in a desert waste...an island in the midst of pirates. The Bedouin tribes are the corsairs of the wilderness..." He even paints an extremely sombre picture of Jerusalem: "a city of ruins. Here and there a regular street, or a well-built European house emerges from the general crash, but the general appearance is that of a city which has been burnt down in some great conflagration." He poses the question: what is the link and what is there in common between Palestine and the people of Israel? His answer is that just as Palestine is isolated and remote, so too are the people of Israel separated and isolated from the other nations; just as Palestine is narrow and small, so too are the people of Israel the smallest of nations; in spite of which, just as the country is thought of as the hub and centre of the universe, so too are the people of Israel regarded as the chosen among the nations.

Stanley also wonders how it is that Palestine was described in the past as "a land of milk and honey". He asks, if in fact is was so, what brought about its later state of desolation and decay? He suggests two possible answers. The first is the destruction of the forests that once covered the country's mountains and the breaking down of the terraces that had conserved the soil. The second are the profound changes that have taken place in the composition of the population and in their culture.

By entitling his preface, "The Connection of Sacred History and Sacred Geography", Stanley reveals his attempt to find geographical grounds for the country's sanctity. In answering his first question he links the history of the Chosen People with the geographical features of the

Promised Land. He seeks the decisive factors of the historical development of Palestine in the framework of its geographical conditions.

Stanley's second question was one that interested many travellers and explorers, both before and after him.

Some godfearing souls attributed the change to God's curse from which there was no appeal. Some explorers accepted the Biblical description of the land as accurate, but could find no explanation for the radical change in the country's physiognomy. Other people postulated that, among other factors, climatic changes brought about the drying up of water sources. Stanley himself suggested changes in social conditions and agricultural methods as the cause of the "revolution". His hypothesis was not far off the mark.

In an appendix to his work, the geographical terms used in the Bible are given in Hebrew with English translations and text references.

The lithographed maps in the book are designed to indicate not only contours but also the character and complexion of the landscape. Thus, purple represents granite and basalt; light red — sandstone; dark green — forest; light green — pasture land; dark yellow — grain; light yellow — sands; brown — desert; grey or white — limestone, saline lands, and snow.

# CHAPTER FOUR

# IN THE WAKE OF
# THE CRIMEAN WAR (1856-1865)
# GREAT INDIVIDUAL EXPLORERS

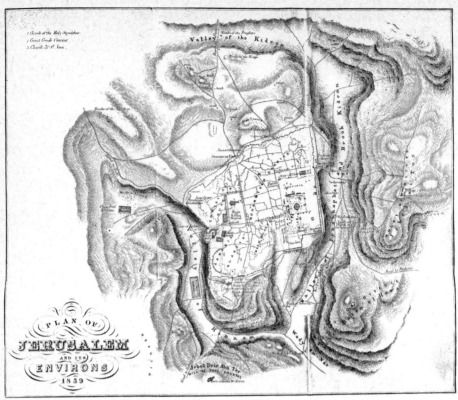

*Plan of Jerusalem and its environs. (Thomson, 1859, p. 602).*

*The Land and the Book or Biblical Illustrations drawn from the Manners and Customs, the Scenes and the Scenery of the Holy Land* was written by the American missionary, W.M. Thomson. It is said that after *Uncle Tom's Cabin* it was the most popular American book of its time. The author continually revised new editions as more information about Syria and Palestine came to light. The above map shows the city as it was when still confined within the walls.

# ADMINISTRATIVE CHANGES
# URBAN DEVELOPMENT

The peace treaty signed between the powers in 1856 on conclusion of the Crimean War regulated, among other matters, the status of the non-Muslim communities in the Ottoman Empire — the rights and duties of the religious authorities, the manner of their election, their salaries, and so on. Turkey, under pressure by the European powers, continued the process of reforms — the Tanzimat. The governor of Jerusalem, in the name of the sultan, ceremoniously proclaimed the edict — the "Hatt-i Hümayun" in 1856 — abolishing discrimination and extending official recognition to all existing faiths. Religious coercion was forbidden and all the sultan's subjects made equal before the law. But despite these declarations and other liberal changes many instances of discrimination still remained in practice.

However, as Turkey's dependence on the European powers grew and the system of capitulations became more entrenched, the situation of the minorities improved, for the powers exploited their administrative and jurisdictional privileges over those residents in the Ottoman Empire who had come under their protection. Every offence against a protected person brought in its wake the forceful intervention of his consul, who saw to it that his country's prestige was upheld. Thousands of Christians and Jews came under the aegis of the British, Austrian, Prussian, Russian, French, and Spanish consular representatives. To the consuls, these protected persons were a means of extending their country's influence in the internal affairs of the Ottoman Empire.

With the growth of European influence organized mass-pilgrimages to Palestine increased — especially from Russia. Following the Crimean War, Russia pushed forward a policy of penetration from within by exhibiting even greater interest in the religious affairs of Palestine. The appointment of high-level ecclesiastical representatives to Jerusalem in 1858, marked the advance of Russian domination over the Greek Orthodox church in the Holy Land. One of the methods employed was the provision of financial aid to Russian pilgrims. The czar himself appealed to all believers to support the pilgrims and a special organisation was set up to take charge of the pilgrims from the moment of their arrival at Jaffa until their return to the ship. Pilgrimages from Russia multiplied especially between Christmas and Easter. In 1860 a great hospice was built for them outside the walls of Jerusalem, and later, a Russian colony was set up in En Karem.

In the following decades, other Christian denominations built churches and monasteries not only to serve the needs of the priests and monks, but also for the accommodation of pilgrims and travellers. At the same time, foreign institutions opened many schools where thousands of children from the various native communities acquired the languages and cultural values of Europe. Russian, French, British, German, Austrian, and Italian post offices were opened; foreign stamps and currencies were used, not only by foreign residents but also by the native population who found these services more reliable than those provided by the government. Although this occurred elsewhere in the Ottoman Empire as well, it was especially marked in Palestine owing to the numerous travellers and tourists requiring these services.

Due largely to the initiative of Sir Moses Montefiore, new developments also occurred in the Jewish community. Land was acquired by him outside the Old City walls and, in 1860, houses were built for the poor with funds left by the Jewish-American philanthropist Judah Touro, of Newport, Rhode Island. This sale of land in Jerusalem to a non-Muslim foreigner created a precedent. Montefiore had already previously bought land occupied by an orange grove near Jaffa. The grove was administered by a German convert to Judaism, who took it upon himself to instruct Jews in agricultural work. By now Jews were immigrating in large numbers. In 1857, Haifa absorbed new Jewish families, and the Jewish population of Jerusalem also increased. In 1854, the Russian government prohibited Jews there from sending funds to Palestine. But after a period of distress for the communities in Jerusalem, Hebron, Safed, and Tiberias, support began to flow in also from West-European Jewish communities and fund-raising for the Jews of Palestine was placed on a sound, organised footing. Clinics, schools, synagogues, and various welfare institutions were set up; the economic conditions of local Jews began to improve.

A new element in the social composition of the local population was introduced in the early 1860's as North African Muslims began settling in towns and villages. This was a result of the Abd-el-Kader revolt against the

*Jérusalem, Vue du Mont des Oliviers. (Van de Velde, 1857).*

Sultan of Morocco and French rule in Algeria, in 1847. After initial successes, Abd-el-Kader was imprisoned in France, but later, in 1852, was exiled to Damascus where he was joined by many Algerian fighting men.

In 1860, a riotous rabble of fanatic Druse, Muslim Arabs, and Kurds ravaged the Christian quarter of Damascus, killing and looting as they went. Abd-el-Kader's men did their best to quell the pogrom but the internecine quarrels that swept Syria and the Lebanon during the following years caused many of the North-African exiles to seek relative peace and quiet in Palestine. Many settled in Safed, forming a considerable part of the Muslim population there. Other emigrants from the Maghreb settled in many of the towns and villages of the country.

Ever since their return in 1840, the Ottoman authorities were bent on the administrative reorganisation of their Palestinian provinces. Until the Egyptian occupation, the country had been divided between the two pashaliks of Damascus and Sidon, giving much latitude to local rulers far removed from central controls. Now, a rigid ruling hierarchy was imposed from Constantinople, with every official fully responsible to his immediate superior — the end of the chain reaching to the Turkish Ministry of the Interior. At every level of government, the Ottoman officials were assisted by a council — "medjlis" — representing the local population through the various "millets" (religious communities) — Muslim, Christian, and others. While the new system did not provide truly representative government, or put an end to corruption, it did minimize arbitrary acts on the part of local governors and gave the religious communities some sort of influence over the affairs immediately affecting them.

Changes were also introduced in the internal divisions of the two "vilayets" of Damascus and Sidon. The country east of Jordan remained part of the Damascus vilayet, but Nablus, Jerusalem, and Gaza were transferred to Sidon, with Beirut assuming importance second only to Damascus as a provincial capital. The Palestinian territories were constituted as a separate entity — "mutasheriflik" — headed by a pasha (mutasherif) responsible to the Porte as well as to the wali of Sidon. In 1854, Jerusalem was made a separate vilayet ruled directly by the central government; other districts, such as Akko, were also eventually granted independent or semi-independent status.

However, none of these administrative changes brought peace and security to the country. The borderlands of the desert and the coastal plain were still subjected to the whims of Bedouin sheikhs who extorted what they could from the hapless villagers and fellaheen. In the mountain regions, local headmen continued much as before, doing as they saw fit. So, for example, the sheikhs of Abu Ghosh continued to levy road tax on all travellers going to Jerusalem. Despite certain improvements in the lives of the inhabitants of the larger towns, there were no appreciable changes in the countryside during the sixties of the last century. Neglect and lack of security were still dominant features of the physical and human landscape of Palestine.


## "AT HOME IN THE HOLY LAND" THROUGH THE EYES OF ITS INHABITANTS

The movement of visitors to Palestine did not cease even during the Crimean War, which had no effect on the security situation in the country.

By now tourists came equipped with cameras, and reproductions of photographs made their appearance in the books they wrote. Local people took to writing about the land they lived in, while growing numbers of visitors from abroad tended to stay longer in the country.

For seventeen years, from 1845 to 1862, James **Finn** served as British consul in Jerusalem, becoming intimately familiar with the country and its people, and particularly friendly with the Jews. Finn was a moving spirit in the social life of Jerusalem's "high society". Among many other activities he founded the Jerusalem Literary Society to record findings and observations and to promote study and research on the country. His reminiscences, *Stirring Times*, were compiled in 1870 and edited and published posthumously, in 1878, by his widow. The book provides detailed descriptions of the Jewish community and of many facets of life in Jerusalem and the surrounding countryside. Finn was fluent in Arabic and Hebrew and had studied Jewish history. Apalled by the degraded condition of the Jews of Jerusalem, he promoted the idea of agricultural work and large-scale Jewish settlement in Palestine, working out a detailed plan for such a project. He also participated in the beginnings of a settlement for Jewish converts to Christianity at Artas village near Solomon's Pools outside Bethlehem. While his interest in the Jews had missionary motivations, Finn extended help fairly and unstintingly. He made himself responsible not only for those Jews who were British subjects, but for Jews in general, upholding their human rights vis-a-vis the Turkish authorities.

**Finn**'s wife, **Elizabeth** Anne, an author in her own right, assisted him fully and survived him by many years. Two of her books *Home in the Holy Land* (1866) and *A Third Year in Jerusalem* (1869), depict customs and incidents of her day. A third, *Reminiscences*, dictated by her in 1913 was only published in 1929, eight years after her death.

Sarah **Barclay**, daughter of an American doctor-missionary, lived in Jerusalem from 1855 to 1857. Of her book *Hadji in Syria or Three Years in Jerusalem*, Titus Tobler remarks that, accurate and accomplished, it is the best book about Palestine written by a woman.

Her father, Dr. James **Barclay** had been commissioned by the sultan to assist a Turkish architect carry out repairs at the Dome of the Rock. This gave him free movement on the Temple Mount for several weeks and enabled him later to record his observations in an interesting book, *The City of the Great King, or Jerusalem as it was, as it is, as it is to be.*

*The Anglican church and British consulate and the Tower of David.*
*(Finn, 1878, II. Frontispiece).*

This coloured lithograph shows the first Anglican church adjoining the British consul's residence inaugurated in Jerusalem on 21 January 1849. The builders had to remove a 40-foot accumulation of rubble before reaching foundation rock. The church is built in neo-Gothic style on a cruciform plan.

Although the work was severely criticised by Tobler and others, on many counts, for presenting unfounded theories and omitting to cite its sources, it does contain new information about contemporary Jerusalem. One of the walled-up gates of the Temple Mount, south of the Wailing Wall, is known to this day as "Barclay's Gate", since it was he who first drew attention to its existence. The gate has been partly uncovered in the recent excavations at the Western Wall.

Another physician to write of his visit to Jerusalem was Dr. Ludwig **Frankl** of Vienna. On behalf of a distinguished Jewish lady, Mrs. Hertz Lemel, he came to establish an almshouse for children. On the way he passed through Greece, Asia Minor, and Syria taking particular interest in the condition of the Jewish communities there. His book, *Nach Jerusalem*, is a valuable source of information on Jewish life in those countries and in Palestine.

Rabbis, scholars, as well as noted explorers like Ritter and Humboldt expressed praise for Israel Joseph **Benjamin**'s *Cinq années de voyage en Orient*, though actually its contribution to knowledge of the East was minimal. The author regarded himself as the second Benjamin of Tudela, the famed medieval Jewish traveller. The work was first published in French in 1856, then in German in 1858, in Hebrew and in English in 1859 under the title *Eight Years in Asia and Africa from 1846 to 1855*.

Another Jewish traveller, Rabbi Ya'aqov Halevi **Sapir**, spent almost five years in extensive travels from Jerusalem via Egypt, the shores of the Red Sea, Yemen, India, and the Pacific islands to Australia, diligently noting down his experiences and impressions, especially of the Jews in Yemen whom he described in his book *Even Sapir*. Before his departure, he had already contributed to knowledge of Palestine in a letter sent to Jewish communities abroad to solicit their purchase of Palestinian "*etrogim*" (citrons) for ritual use in the Succoth festival, the Feast of Tabernacles. His letter gives a lively description of agricultural practices in the area around Umm-el-Fahm.

Another woman writer was Mary Eliza **Rogers**, whose brother Edward served on the staff of the British consulate in Jerusalem in the years 1848—1853. Her *Domestic Life in Palestine*, is based on first-hand experience for she lived in the country for nearly twenty-five years, between 1835 and 1859, earning a well-deserved reputation as an authority on the landscape and folkways of Palestine.

165

*Israel Joseph Benjamin ("The Second"). (Benjamin, 1865).*

In his youth Benjamin "the Second" traded in wood and grain, but, after losing his fortune, decided to fulfill an early ambition and travel in the East, to observe the life of the Jews in the hope of finding traces of the ten lost tribes. In 1856 he left his homeland, Rumania. It took him two years to reach Palestine, where he stayed six months, going on later to other Asian countries and to North Africa. He adopted the pen-name of "Benjamin the Second", considering himself the successor of the famous 12th century Jewish traveller, Benjamin of Tudela.

One of the most popular writers on the country at this time was John L. **Porter**. Although unscientific in his approach, Porter was a good, intelligent observer who resided many years in Syria and Palestine. His long stay in the East resulted in many publications rich in details and descriptions of the whole of Palestine, including a very popular pocket tourist guide book published in the *J. Murray's Handbook* series, issued in 1858. This handy little book was one of the earliest such vademecums of Palestine, being reprinted many times. Later, in the eighties, two finely illustrated books by Porter appeared, both with explanatory texts on his travels in Palestine. Porter also maintained close contacts with the Paul Lortet expedition that explored parts of the country in the years 1875 to 1880.

The Reverend W.M. **Thomson** reputedly made more journeys than any other individual explorer or visitor of the 19th century in Palestine. This American missionary lived and worked in the region for many years, from 1833 until 1879 or so. During this time he came to know Palestine through and through. As mentioned above, Thomson was chosen by Robinson to accompany him during part of the latter's second visit. Thomson describes his work, *The Land and the Book*, as popular in character and not intended for the scholar; his main purpose being to describe the country in reference to the Bible, much of the text dealing with the folklore of Palestine in illustration of Biblical ways. *The Land and the Book* was issued and re-issued in tens of editions and a variety of formats and bindings, serving as a favourite end-of-term prize for generations of Sunday-school pupils.

Among the many other travellers in the years between 1853 and 1860, were the Prussian consul August **Petermann** who wrote *Reisen im Orient* and William **Beaumont**, author of *A Diary of a Journey to the East...* and of *Cairo to Sinai and Sinai to Cairo 1860—1861*. Tobler speaks of the valuable observations in the first; the second has no material on Palestine but there is an interesting chapter on Bedouin ways. Robert **Stewart's** *The Tent and the Khan, a Journey to Sinai and Palestine*, is one of the better and more original works by ordinary travellers. Horatio **Bonar's** *The Desert of Sinai; a Spring Journey from Cairo to Beersheba* and *The Land of Promise; Notes of a Spring Journey from Beersheba to Sidon*, each with a map showing the routes followed by him; and the works of H.S. **Osborn**, G.M. **Wortabet**, W. **Ritchie**, Felix **Bovet**, and F. **Bremer**, were but a few of a plethora of works by a host of travellers, each of whom

167

*Khan et Tejjar — Arab fair (Thomson, 1859, p. 152).*

Thomson's book is profusely illustrated, but his pictures are not original, having often appeared in other books. Many were taken from Van de Velde, but the copies are inferior. The above is reworked from one of Bartlett's pictures in Stebbing's book. It shows the merchants's khan near Mt. Tabor.

must have been certain that his contribution to the voluminous travel literature of the age was indispensable.

A sentence in Lord **Lindsay**'s introduction to the fifth edition of his book (1858) is a fitting summing-up of the mid-century contributors to the exploration of Palestine. Because so much had been added to Palestine exploration since his first visit in 1837, he regrets that he made that journey at a time when knowledge of the country was still so meagre.

If the fifties of the 19th century saw a growing number of individual researchers who spent some time in the country, the sixties witnessed the coming of age of explorations by important expeditions using scientific methods and modern equipment.


# THE ROYAL EXPEDITIONS
# REALISTIC WRITERS

The scientific approach of Ernest **Renan**, who was sent by Napoleon III to head an archaeological mission in 1860 to explore Phoenicia, was a turning-point in the study of Palestine's past, even though his own part in the uncovering of the historical finds of Western Palestine was limited.

The French expedition excavated the ruins of Jebal, Tyre, and Sidon, revealing mainly remains of the Hellenistic-Roman period. This work made Renan the first to carry out archaeological excavations in the region. His arrival in the Lebanon coincided with the end of the massacres of Christians by Druse, which led to the military occupation of Lebanon by France and her domination of the region. Welcomed by the Lebanese Christians as a saviour, Renan enjoyed their full assistance. He was also helped in the excavations by French troops, while the French fleet provided transport for the personnel and the finds. Resident French citizens, surveyors, and architects also helped.

Renan stayed in the Lebanon for a year until October 1861. During this time he visited Palestine — which he regarded as part of "his" Phoenicia — and discovered remains of ancient synagogues in Galilee.

A year later in 1861—1862, sixteen years after Lynch's celebrated investigations, the Duc de **Luynes** organised a new expedition to explore

169

the Dead Sea and its vicinity, but covering a much larger area than Lynch, and making extensive excursions to the regions of Amman and Moab, the Arava as far as the Gulf of Aqaba, and to the ruins of Petra. Some of the members made supplementary journeys, such as that by L. de **Vignes**, who commanded the exploration vessel on the Dead Sea, to Palmyra; and by the French architect in Jerusalem, C. **Mauss**, who went to Kerak and Shaubek. Vignes and Mauss, as well as the geologist L. **Lartet**, added their own accounts to the report of the expedition, published in three volumes, an atlas, and pictures. Lartet's article, later issued separately in book form, proved a most valuable contribution to Palestine geology in general, and to the geology of the Jordan Rift and the Dead Sea in particular. He wrote that from a physical point of view, Palestine, at the time of his visit, was as unknown as the deserts of Africa and Central Asia. The Duc de Luynes's expedition drew attention, for the first time, to prehistoric flint tools in Syria and Palestine.

Because of de Luynes's untimely death, the expedition's journals were edited by the Comte Melchior de **Vogüé**, known for his architectural studies of Jerusalem and its surroundings. Beginning in 1854 with the Church of the Holy Sepulchre, the Basilica of the Nativity in Bethlehem, and other churches, he made exploratory journeys in the area of the Horan in North Syria and then resumed work in Jerusalem in 1861. De Vogüé, greatly helped by the epigrapher Waddington, devoted himself to studying the Temple Mount. The results of his research appeared in two magnificently illustrated books, one on the churches of the Holy Land, the other on the Temple at Jerusalem. His book, in three parts, *La Syrie centrale*, was widely acclaimed for its information on the antiquities of that region. Another work included excerpts from his travel diary.

The next expedition was of a different character. It was a royal tour under the Prince of Wales, later to become King Edward VII. The Palestine excursion was part of a mission by the prince to Egypt, Syria, Turkey, Greece, and the Mediterranean islands. He was accompanied by Dean A.P. Stanley as scientific adviser and by the photographer Francis **Bedford**. Bedford's photographs — with accompanying text by W.M. Thomson — revealed the true landscape of the country, including hitherto hidden corners and subjects previously distorted by overly imaginary or emotional vision. The album, in large format, containing 182 of Bedford's photographs that had been exhibited to the public, was so expensive that a cheaper edition was published with 48 photographs and text by

*Jerusalem — 1864. (de Luynes, Atlas, 1871—6, plate 24).*

The report of the Duc de Luynes expedition appeared in a magnificent production. De Luynes died suddenly and it was completed by the Comte de Vogüé. The work includes an atlas, with maps and photographs prepared by members of the expedition. The photographs — including the one above — were among the first taken in the country.

*Naplouse (Nablus — Shechem) 1864. (De Luynes, Atlas
1871-6, plate 20).*

In mid-19th century Nablus was only second to Jerusalem in importance with a population of about 10,000. The town occupied an area of about 1,000 by 500 metres
extending over the entire width of the valley between Mt. Gerizim and Mt. Ebal.
The town nestled among the trees and foliage and springs in the area provided a good
water supply. The town's wall was broken, the many breaches being stopped up by the
walls of houses and stone fences. Wayfarers were intrigued with the magnificent
market places of Nablus. Many of the visitors describe the ancient Samaritan sect and
also the small Jewish community there. This view, one of the first photographs of
Nablus, was taken by the de Luynes expedition and appears in his atlas.

172

*Pool of Mamillah, west of the city. (Pierotti, 1864, II).*

Between 1854 and 1864 an Italian engineer, E. Pierotti, was employed by the Turkish government in Jerusalem. The book he produced contained many views of sites in the city accompanied by detailed explanations. The following places are indicated by number in the picture above:

1. The Russian compound; 2. The north-west corner of the wall; 3. The city wall; 4. The Mount of Olives; 5. The road to the Monastery of the Cross; 6. The Muslim cemetery; 7. An ancient Saracen monument; 8. Pool of Mamillah.

173

*View of the Coenaculum, and of the so-called Tomb of David.*
*(Pierotti, 1864, II, plate XLV).*

Warren and Wilson's work superseded Pierotti's *Jerusalem Explored* in learned opinion. Warren took a dim view of some of Pierotti's identifications of ancient sites. But despite the criticism, Pierotti's work is impressive in its beauty. In the margins of the picture he explains the different parts of the scenes. For example, in this view of David's Tomb and Mount Zion, the faintly visible numbers denote: 1. the main church; 2. Arab houses; 3. the Coenaculum — the room of the Last Supper; 4. the dome of David's Tomb; 5. modern Arab houses; 6. the Christian cemetery. Another interesting illustration is of the city wall near the Jaffa Gate before it was breached for Kaiser Wilhelm's visit in 1898.

Thomson. Among the pictures is one of the Absalom and Zachariah monuments in the Valley of Jehoshaphat, showing that the Jewish cemetery on the Mount of Olives extended at that time to the bottom of the Kidron Valley. The original photographs, which were deposited in the British Museum, were destroyed by German bombs in the second world war.

The Prince of Wales's visit to the Tomb of the Patriarchs in Hebron set a precedent followed by other royal visitors who obtained special firmans from the sultan, though to other non-Muslims — with very few exceptions — it remained forbidden ground until the first world war.

A.P. **Stanley** now brought out a revised edition of *Sinai and Palestine*, writing in the introduction that "In these same nine years (since his first visit) the geography of Palestine has been almost rewritten. Not only have new discoveries been made in every part, but the historical and topographical details of the subject have been worked up into a far more complete form.

De **Saulcy**, who was mentioned already in connection with his explorations in the Dead Sea region in 1851—52, was the first to engage in archaeological excavations in Western Palestine proper, receiving a permit in 1863 from the Ottoman government to excavate at the Tomb of the Kings in Jerusalem. His unscientific methods were more like a treasure hunt, though he did discover several decorated sarcophagi, one of them with a two-line inscription reading *"Tzedek Malkhata"* and *"Tzedah Malkhata"*. We know now that this refers to Queen Helena of Adiabene who adopted Judaism in the first century C.E., and that the tomb is that of her family. As de Saulcy was unacquainted with the Aramaic script of the Second Temple period he assumed that the inscription was in ancient Hebrew and referred to the wife of Zedekiah, King of Judah. His second visit resulted in two more books; one, on his travels in the Holy Land, and the other on the "Tombs of the Kings" and other sites. In 1877 he wrote *Holy Land*, a lexicon of Biblical geography, and in 1881 *Jerusalem*, a "summary" book of sketches and maps.

Among the writers who visited Palestine early in the sixties was F. **Frith**, who published one of the first collections of landscape photographs of Palestine with the actual photographs pasted into the book for lack of better techniques of reproduction. Frith argues the importance of using photographs to give a true picture of the country; T. **Lewin's** *The Siege*

175

*of Jerusalem by Titus*, has a chapter on the author's journey in 1862 to Jerusalem, the Jordan Rift area and the Dead Sea; Mrs. Mentor **Mott**, whose little book also contains photographs by Francis Bedford; and N. **Macleod**, a Scottish preacher who, along with others, is singled out in Montefiore's diary for slandering the Jews of Safed, are some of the other authors of these years. **Van de Velde**'s revised edition of his map appeared following a second visit in 1861—1862. The new map gives new soundings along the Mediterranean coast and some 1,800 place-names, mainly in Western Palestine.

Hebrew writings, too, which began to appear in Palestine in the sixties made an important contribution to the knowledge of the country. Among them were the first Hebrew weeklies, *"ha-Levanon"* and *"ha-Havatzelet"*, as well as letters and memoirs by leaders of the Jerusalem community.

Now that the Age of Romanticism had given way to more materialistic times, there also appeared travellers who did not shrink from showing the country in all its wretchedness. One such, William H. **Dixon**, gives lively descriptions of life in Palestine's towns and villages. In the introduction to his book, Dixon writes that he deals with the "landscapes and the politics of the Holy Land", and that it was written in tent, khan, and sitting on the ground, in the form of letters sent home to his friends for their entertainment around the fireplace. He reports faithfully what he saw and heard. Dixon's book is important for the no-nonsense, straightforward descriptions of the country at the time of his visit in about 1864.

Samuel L. **Clemens**, better known as Mark Twain, made the Grand Tour of Europe and the East in 1867, immortalizing his impressions to the delight of his readers in *The Innocents Abroad, or the New Pilgrim's Progress*. But Mark Twain was clearly jarred by the dismal state of the Holy Land and his humour here is tinged by bitterness. A sample of his impressions speaks for itself.

> ...As we rode into Magdala not a soul was visible. But the ring of the horses' hoofs roused the stupid population, and they all came trooping out — old men and old women, boys and girls, the blind, the crazy, and the crippled, all in ragged, soiled and scanty raiment, and all abject beggars by nature, instinct and education. How the vermin-tortured vagabonds did swarm! How they showed their scars and sores, and piteously pointed to their maimed and crooked limbs, and begged with their pleading eyes for charity! We had invoked a spirit we could not lay. They hung to the horses's tails, clung to their manes and the stirrups, closed in on every side in scorn of dangerous hoofs — and out

176

of their infidel throats, with one accord, burst an agonizing and most infernal chorus: "Howajji, bucksheesh! howajji, bucksheesh! howajji, bucksheesh! bucksheesh! bucksheesh!" I was never in a storm like that before.

# LEADING PERSONALITIES: MAJOR CONTRIBUTIONS

Titus **Tobler**'s third visit to Palestine resulted in *Dritte Wanderung nach Palästina im Jahre 1857*, which added much of interest on Jerusalem. In 1865, thirty years after his first journey, came his fourth visit, the purpose of which was to explore Nazareth. He wrote a monograph on the town, making expert use of the literary material available. Tobler also compiled a comprehensive, critical bibliography of Palestine geography in three parts: travellers's accounts, summaries by authors who had not themselves visited the country, and pictures and maps, listing over 1,500 scientists, travellers, cartographers, and others who contributed to an understanding of the historical geography of Palestine up to 1865. Until his death in 1877, this learned explorer continued working on studies of Palestine and editing ancient pilgrims' texts.

Much has been written about Henry Baker **Tristram**, who first visited Palestine at the end of the fifties. In 1857 and 1858, while on a Mediterranean cruise, he spent two months in the country — but only in the Jaffa and Jerusalem areas, though from this brief stay he was able to write an article for the journal, *The Ibis*, with observations on the fauna of Palestine. To his surprise, Tristram found how little was known about the country's animal and plant life — much less than about the same subjects in other countries of travel. He suggests two reasons for this neglect: the concentration of inquiries on historical and religious aspects, and the difficulties and dangers of a region so desolate and wild. In this first report, Tristram gives a brief list of rare birds observed by him during his short stay. In preparing material for William Smith's *Dictionary of the Bible*, it became clear to Tristram that for the correct rendering of the Biblical names of animals and plants, much information had to be gathered and that an understanding of the many problems, both biological and geographical, arising from the investigation of the desert, required a basic study of the natural conditions of the country. In dealing with the fish of Lake Kinneret, for example, he could not find any reliable and exact data. He was convinced that many interesting discoveries awaited the researcher of this lake, since the Jordan is an inland river with no outlet to the Mediterranean.

Tristram prepared himself for his mission by defining the problems and advancing tentative theories, and also by acquiring some instruction in geological surveying methods.

His opportunity came when the Society for Promoting Christian Knowledge invited him to write a book on the Holy Land. September 1863 found him in Beirut recruiting a small group of biologists and divinity students. Then, Bible in hand, they traversed the country collecting specimens and always keeping the question in mind that had intrigued their predecessors: is there any difference between the Palestine of the 19th century and that described in the Scriptures? Their conclusions were that what the Bible tells of the country's natural and geographical conditions, in no way differed from those of the present, thus verifying for them the reliability of the Holy Writ.

Tristram's route wound from Beirut by way of Rosh Haniqra to Akko, and after visiting Nahal Keziv (Wadi Qarn), the party proceeded to Jenin and on to Jerusalem. The winter was passed in Jericho and the Jordan Valley. He relates how he used to sit in front of his open tent; on the table before him were spread the skins of sunbirds, kingfishers, swallows, and other birds, while his companions and the Arabs of the neighbourhood brought him a constant supply of fowls and other creatures to identify and record.

Tristram continued his explorations in the Northern Negev, Gilead, and Galilee; returning via Jerusalem to Nazareth, Syria, and Beirut.

The fruit of this journey was Tristram's *The Land of Israel, a Journal of Travels in Palestine* and a number of other publications. A later trip through Transjordan, resulted in *The Land of Moab...* Other works by Tristram are *Bible Places or the Topography of the Holy Land; a succinct account of all the places, rivers and mountains mentioned in the Bible* (1872), *Pathways of Palestine...* (1881—2); and *The Fauna and Flora of Palestine* (1884). This latter, which is undoubtedly the foundation stone of Palestine biological research, was one of the volumes of the Palestine Exploration Fund's *Survey of Western Palestine*. A later work, *Eastern*

178

*Portrait of Henry Baker Tristram — zoologist and author.*
*(Palestine Exploration Fund photograph).*

Canon Tristram had vast knowledge in many fields but was mainly known as a student of nature, earning for himself the title of father of Palestine zoology. Tristram devoted special attention to ornithology. He first travelled in Palestine in 1857, and although he concentrated on its physical aspects, did not neglect other fields. In the introduction to his *The Land of Israel* Tristram points out that every country in the world evokes a desire to know it better, but Palestine is of special interest because of its ancient past and the sacred events that occurred there.

179

*Wady (ruins) Zuweirah. (Metzad Zohar). (Tristram 1865, p. 352).*

Tristram's first journey in Palestine was undertaken in 1863-1864. His team never consisted of more than six men; and most of the time it included a photographer, artist, botanist, and zoologist. The expedition to the Dead Sea in 1864 required a caravan of 43 animals to carry the baggage. Tristram did not consider this as unduly large, but he did remark that the Duc de Luynes expedition, which preceded him in exploring the Dead Sea area, was extravagant in both size and cost.

*Khan and bridge over the Jordan. (Tristram, 1865, p. 445).*

Many excellent illustrations embellished Tristram's work which contains also a handsome lithographed map, in colour, of Palestine and the Dead Sea showing the routes he took. Although there was a photographer in the expedition, there are no photographs in his first book *The Land of Israel*. Tristram tells of having cameras repaired in Jerusalem and it is possible that the photographs were used when preparing the illustrations for publication, which may account for their great accuracy.

*Plain of Gennesaret. (Tristram, 1866, p. 432).*

"Many travelled the country and wrote about it", says Tristram, referring particularly to Robinson and Stanley, but he believed there was much more to be done. He wanted to concentrate on the physical aspects of Palestine (biology and geology) and to explore lesser-known regions of the Dead Sea and the areas east of the Jordan. But he gave much attention to other areas too: spending about ten days studying the shores of the Sea of Galilee and three weeks exploring the area between it and the southern slopes of Mount Hermon. The illustration shows the Plain of Gennesaret during his visit — a stretch of flat land, abandoned and dotted with bushes and thorns.

182

*Customs in the Bible Lands* (1894), is evidence of Tristram's vast range of interests.

Victor **Guérin's** seven great volumes rival in scope the publications of the Palestine Exploration Fund — an astonishing achievement for one man. Guérin first visited Palestine in 1852, when Robinson was there for the second time, and his last visit, in 1875, coincided with the Palestine Exploration Fund's intensive survey. Although Tobler was in Palestine at the same time they never met there.

Like Robinson, Guérin tried to identify Biblical sites from the existing landscape. His map of 1863 superseded that of Kiepert and Robinson, both archaeologically and topographically. The importance of Guérin's work lies in the vast amount of material it embodies on the Palestine of his day. From an archaeological point of view, he failed to grasp that the country's many tels cover the sites of ancient cities. It is therefore difficult to regard his finds as modern archaeological evidence, or to consider his work as a scientific document. All the same, Guérin is to be credited with having examined the Hasmonean tombs at Modi'in, and uncovering a number of ancient synagogues in Galilee.

He visited Palestine five times. In 1852 he travelled along the main roads, while in 1854 he left the usual routes to traverse the length and breadth of the country. The results of these two journeys are given in his first book. His three main visits, in 1863, 1870, and 1875, were made on behalf of the Turkish Ministry of Public Works.

Although his writings are in the form of a diary, Guérin does not speak of his personal experiences except to underscore or demonstrate a particular point. The publications of the Palestine Exploration Fund draw on much of his material, but the two are not always in agreement. Sometimes where Guérin is detailed, the P.E.F. deals with the same subject only cursorily, and vice versa — apparently reflecting a different evaluation. In fact, Guérin's great work and that of the P.E.F. complement one another.

Translating scientific work is obviously best done by an authority on the subject, familiar with the material. He should also be able, if necessary, to bring the work up to date. These qualities were admirably exhibited by William F. **Gage**, who in 1864 condensed and translated parts of Carl Ritter's monumental work. Gage's edition, *The Comparative Geography of Palestine and the Sinaitic Peninsula*, in four volumes, also contains the literary sources dealing with the exploration of Palestine, a re-evaluation of these sources, Tobler's bibliography, Tristram's report on Bet She'an and other matters.

Works summing-up existing knowledge on Palestine proliferated in the fifties and sixties of the century. After Gage's translation of Ritter there appeared the *Biblical Dictionary* of William **Smith** and George **Grove**. The latter, who contributed "A Vocabulary of the Chief Topographical and Geographical Words used in Scripture" as an appendix to Stanley's *Sinai and Palestine*, took it upon himself to write articles on the country, visiting Palestine for this purpose in 1858. His articles earned high praise for their insight and accuracy. His visit convinced Grove of the urgent need for a new, reliable map of Palestine. Not a cartographer himself, he confined himself to a study of the past history of Palestine, in which he joined with his friend James **Fergusson**, an architect who had studied the topography of Jerusalem and published a controversial book propounding original ideas that located the Church of the Holy Sepulchre within the area of the Temple Mount.

In 1868 Smith and Grove published a Biblical atlas covering the ancient, Biblical, and classical geography of Palestine. The index by Grove contained all the geographical names in the Bible. Several revised editions of the atlas were produced subsequently.

A year after the publication of Smith and Grove's dictionary, the first scientific mapping of Jerusalem was undertaken, motivated largely by the serious shortage of water in the city. John **Whitty**'s article on Jerusalem's water supply was published in the *Journal of Sacred Literature* in London, in 1864. The issue also contains interesting details about Syrian agriculture and cotton growing. Funds for the survey were provided by Lady Burdett-Coutts and other English philanthropists, and the survey itself was carried out by men of the Royal Engineers, under a young officer, Charles **Wilson**. The work took eleven months and was completed in May 1865.

Having at the same time acquired new knowledge of Jerusalem's antiquities, Wilson had his material published a year later in the British War Office's *Ordnance Survey of Jerusalem* in three volumes, with sketch plans and photographs. The first volume has an introduction and a general review of the geology, topography, and water sources, maps of the city and its vicinity, plans of buildings, and other matters relating to

184

a general description of Jerusalem. The second volume is a collection of forty-three pictures of Jerusalem — its walls, gates, buildings, etc., while the third volume contains notes and plans. The *Survey* contains accurate altitude measurements along the road from Jaffa to Jerusalem and from Jerusalem to Solomon's Pools and the Dead Sea. An accurate map of the city to a scale of 1:2,500, and of its surroundings at 1:10,000 also appears in the *Survey*.

On completion of the survey, Wilson took part in the exploration of Jerusalem that was then being carried out on behalf of the Palestine Exploration Fund. He and his colleague, Charles **Warren**, who later headed the Fund's highly successful archaeological expedition, wrote *The Recovery of Jerusalem*.

*The Redjom-El-Mezorrhel, Dead Sea and mountains of Moab.*
*(Isaacs, 1857, p. 20).*

When in the 1850's the camera began to be used in Palestine, its advantages over pencil and brush were not immediately apparent. Photographs were regarded at first merely as a means of providing exact pictures. Artists felt that "subjective" drawings were superior to "objective" photographs. One of those who made use of the camera was the Reverend A.A. Isaacs who visited Palestine in 1856-1857, mainly in order to examine de Saulcy's identification of the sites of Sodom and Gomorrah. The above view, prepared from photographs, shows the ruins of an ancient fort at the northern extremity of Mt. Sodom on the Dead Sea shore.

186

*Gaza. (Neale, 1851—2. Frontispiece).*

It has been claimed that Gaza, at the beginning of the 19th century, was bigger than Jerusalem. With an estimated population of 10,000, Gaza was one of Palestine's principal trading centres. But the depredations of Napoleon and Ibrahim Pasha depopulated the town and arrested its development. After mid-century, however, the population of Gaza increased rapidly and its economy recovered. Visitors describe it as standing amid olive groves in the sand dunes. It is spoken of as a desert port, with a khan where camels could be hired or watered, food and travel necessities purchased, and charcoal obtained. The quarantine establishment shown here was constructed by the Turkish government in 1850. It is a large rectangular compound with storerooms, baths, and fumigation rooms as well as fairly comfortable apartments for travellers who were detained there in an effort to keep plague epidemics out of the country. Gaza appears on a rise in the background.

187

*Coupe d'une excavation isolée à Beit-Jibrin. (Rey, 1859).*

This illustration, (in colour), shows a typical cave in the Beit Jibrin (Beit Guvrin) area. The picture appears in *Etude historique et topographique de la tribu de Juda* by the French explorer E.G. Rey. The book also contains other illustrations of the area as well as valuable maps of Judea and the South. Rey was in Palestine between 1857 and 1858 and published another book, *Voyage dans le Haouran et aux bords de la Mer Morte exécuté pendant les années 1857 et 1858.*

CHAPTER FIVE

# THE BEGINNINGS OF MODERNIZATION (1865-1877)

## EXPLORATION FUNDS AND SCIENTIFIC TEAMS

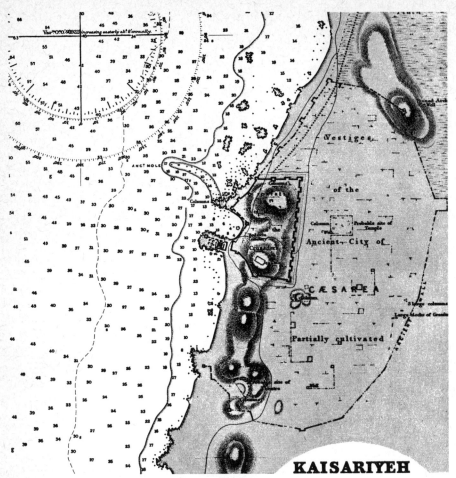

**KAISARIYEH**

*The Anchorage of Caesarea and surrounding coastal plain. (Mansell, 1862).*

In 1862 A.L. Mansell completed his admirable survey of the coast from el Arish to Rosh Hanikra to a scale of 1:243,333. Sea depths are noted in fathoms. Mansell also produced a series of maps of anchorages along the coast on a larger scale — Acre, Haifa Bay, Jaffa, Caesarea (see illustration), and the vicinity of Yavneh. In the margins of some of these there are beautiful steel engravings of landscapes as seen from the sea, to assist navigators in identifying their position. These panoramic strips are typical of 18th and 19th century maps and are sometimes found in maps of this type today. Mansell's maps remained the basis for all coastal surveying in Palestine until the days of the British Mandate.

190

# WESTERN PENETRATION INTENSIFIED
# NEW SETTLEMENTS

The year 1865 marks the opening of the final chapter of our story, not because of any focal political event but because it was then that the Palestine Exploration Fund was established.

The reigns of Sultans Abdul Majid (1839—1861) and Abdul Aziz (1861—1876) saw only little change in the general condition of the Ottoman Empire. But with the accession of Abdul Hamid II economic disintegration quickened, and, at the same time, marked changes occurred in the empire — and especially in Palestine — coming partly in the wake of political events in Europe following the Franco-Prussian war.

During the second half of the 19th century, conditions in Palestine were subjected to strong foreign political influences by means of the consuls, the capitulations, and the technological advances in communication that drew the Ottoman Empire closer to Europe.

At the beginning of the fifties, the large shipping companies, the Austrian Lloyd and the French Messageries Maritimes had begun to call at Palestine ports. Their passenger steam vessels being faster, safer, and more comfortable than sailing ships, tourism to the Holy Land began to increase dramatically. The opening of the Suez Canal in 1869 which brought the Middle East nearer to the Western world also had some influence on the modernization of Palestine. But Palestine did not benefit from the peace and the ensuing prosperity in Syria and Lebanon at the beginning of the sixties when hostilities there between the Druse and the Christians ended. Construction by the French of the port of Beirut — soon to become the main Levant harbour — diverted trade from the roadsteads of Palestine. In 1863, the first carriage road in all Syria was built to connect Beirut with Damascus, and for several decades the wholesale trade of the entire area, including Palestine, passed along it to the new port. Akko, which had in the interval gradually recovered from the destruction wreaked upon it at the time of Ibrahim Pasha's retreat, now declined, never to be revived. Only in Jaffa, the port nearest Jerusalem, was there some improvement in the volume of coastal traffic and in the movement of pilgrims and tourists. The worst blow however was suffered by Gaza, which at the beginning of the century had been Palestine's main commercial and industrial centre.

Nevertheless, the process of modernization continued. In 1865 the first telegraph office opened in Jerusalem. Later, tax reforms were introduced and foreigners were permitted to acquire land on condition that they submitted to Ottoman laws. In 1869, the road between Jaffa and Jerusalem was paved in time to be used by the Austrian Emperor Franz Josef and other royal tourists when they visited Jerusalem after the inauguration festivities of the Suez Canal. But within two years, the road deteriorated and was only resurfaced in 1881 to become Palestine's first metalled carriage way.

Although the capitulations interfered with the normal development of the country, they afforded foreign subjects, and to a certain extent also local citizens, protection from the corruption of the administration and the capriciousness of local officials. The Christians exploited their special status to build churches, monasteries, and social institutions, while the Jews, under the benevolent eye of the foreign powers, set up their first settlement projects.

Jerusalem in particular absorbed influences from the outside which altered its age-old way of life. Hygiene in the Holy City had been no better than in the remotest villages. Jerusalem was steeped in mire and filth; its streets were strewn with animal carcases and slaughter-house offal; refuse piled up around the houses and noisome smells arose from every corner. Were it not for the initiative of foreign residents, this situation would doubtless have continued to befoul the sanctity of the Holy City throughout the sixties as well. But enlightened complaints led to the establishment of a sanitation committee which instituted daily clean-up rounds and installed some lighting in the streets. Similar improvements were carried out in Jaffa where the pilgrim and tourist traffic brought in trade and a demand for services. Many of the country's inhabitants found employment in Christian institutions, while financial assistance from abroad to the Jewish community contributed to the advancement of the country's economy.

After the Crimean War there was a considerable increase in the number of Jews who came to the Land of Israel, many of them motivated by their faith to spend their last years in the Holy Land. Since they were

192

largely supported by charitable donations from pious Jews abroad, they could somehow subsist under the difficult conditions of the country, while those who had greater initiative used some of the incoming funds for attempts at urban and rural settlement. New suburbs rose outside the walls of Old Jerusalem, while in the vicinity of Jaffa, the Miqve Yisra'el agricultural school was set up in 1870 under the able direction of Karl Netter by the Alliance Israélite Association. Although attempts to establish agricultural settlements at Motza, near Jerusalem, and elsewhere were unsuccessful, the idea persisted and others were initiated.

In keeping with its growing numbers, the influence of the Jewish community increased. The Jews now became a majority in Jerusalem, and have remained so ever since. Apart from the old religious schools and academies, new general educational institutions were set up with funds from abroad. The first Hebrew weekly journals were founded.

Several Christian Millenarian and fundamentalist groups also started settlements in the Holy Land. In 1867, members of the Gesellschaft des Tempels, originally from Württemberg in South Germany, took up land in the Arab village of Simoniya in the Jezreel Valley but malaria caused this attempt to be abandoned. A year later, some 160 Millenarians from the United States, under the influence of a mystic named Adams, settled in Jaffa and set up a Church of the Messiah. Differences and quarrels broke out among them, causing the return of part of the group to America. Of the remainder, some joined the first "American Colony" in Jerusalem, while others went over to the German Templars who had begun to establish agricultural communities near some of the larger towns.

Despite liberal-sounding proclamations, the Turkish authorities put many difficulties in the path of these Christian settlers, caring nothing for the modern improvements they introduced to the country's primitive agriculture. The customary Ottoman dilatoriness, however, enabled the European powers to deepen their influence. Such measures as the authorities did take were designed to counteract the mass Christian pilgrimages by encouraging gatherings of Muslims for the Hadj to Mecca and, to coincide with Easter, an annual Moslem pilgrimage to the Dome of the Rock and the shrine at Nebi Musa between Jerusalem and Jericho were instituted. They also settled Muslims from abroad in the country: Circassians from Russia, Moghrabis from North Africa, and Bosnians from the Balkans, and pressed some Bedouins into permanent settlement.

*The German Colony in Haifa. (Geikie, 1882, p. 773).*

In 1869 the fundamentalist German Templars established the agricultural settlement of Sarona near Jaffa and elsewhere, but most of the Templars and some other European immigrants preferred to live in the suburbs they built on the outskirts of the cities, particularly near Jerusalem and Haifa. At the beginning of the eighties there were about a thousand Europeans in these settlements and at the end of the century their number had increased to 1,300. As can be seen from the above illustration, these suburbs still retain much of their original character today.

194

Although this occurred mostly in the last quarter of the 19th century, the process was begun in the years 1865 to 1878.

# THE PALESTINE EXPLORATION FUND: INITIAL OPERATIONS

Two unsuccessful attempts preceded the foundation of the Palestine Exploration Fund in 1865. In 1804, the Palestine Association was formed in London, but did little. In 1810, it published a short report on the areas adjacent to Lake Kinneret, the Jordan, and the Dead Sea, with a map of Palestine — mainly a translation of material Seetzen had sent to the society after his visit to Palestine in 1806. A two-man mission was dispatched to Palestine, but did not get beyond Malta, returning home when they heard rumours of threats to foreigners in Palestine. The Society did nothing further until 1834, when it dissolved itself and transferred its funds, books, and papers to the newly-formed Royal Geographical Society. A second attempt was made in 1840 with the founding of a new society preserving the old name and aims. After producing a few unimportant publications it amalgamated with the Syro-Egyptian Society to form the Biblical Archaeological Society.

Stanley, Tristram, Grove, and several other distinguished explorers took the initiative in the establishment of the Palestine Exploration Fund (P.E.F.), being convinced by Captain Wilson's mapping and reports on Jerusalem that organized scientific work could achieve far more than the efforts of individuals.

The founding meeting of the P.E.F. took place on 12 May 1865 in the "Jerusalem Room" of Westminster Cathedral. It proclaimed the aims of the Palestine Exploration Fund to be the investigation of the archaeology, geography, geology, and natural history — botany, zoology, meteorology — of Palestine. Queen Victoria bestowed her patronage on the Fund and members of the aristocracy, church dignitaries, and public figures joined its Committee. From the outset, the P.E.F. enjoyed considerable public interest and support. At the first meeting of the P.E.F. in 1865, Captain Charles Wilson, just back from Jerusalem, presented proposals for an immediate programme. A reconnaissance

*The first logotype of the Palestine Exploration Fund. (Conder, Tent Work, 1878).*

The Palestine Exploration Fund was founded in London in the year 1865. The Society adopted three basic principles: 1. that its projects be carried out on scientific principles; 2. that the Fund, as a body, abstain from controversy; 3. not to conduct its affairs as a religious body.

The logo of the Society, which appeared in its first publication, shows the method of mapping and the means used in those days — triangulation points and theodolite.

196

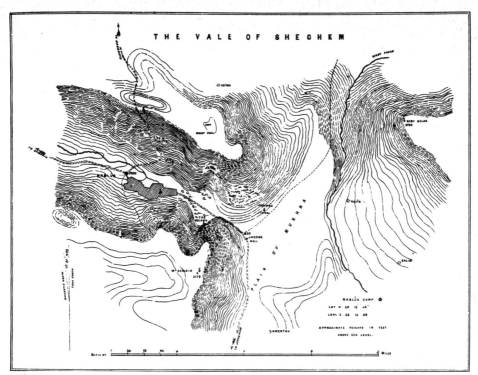

*The vale of Shechem — 1865. (Wilson and Warren, Recovery, 1871).*

Three maps to a scale of 1:160,000 depicting the Sea of Galilee (Lake Kinneret), the Hulah Valley, and the vale of Shekhem were part of the Palestine Exploration Fund's first survey. Although fragmentary, the maps were of great significance as they were the first contour maps ever made of the country and provided experience in topographical measurement — levelling and astronomical determination.

197

mission was to explore parts of Palestine and, depending on the results would make recommendations for the exploration and mapping of the entire country. Wilson was to head the mission with Lieutenant Anderson as his assistant.

The expedition, composed of men of the Royal Engineers, began that same year by mapping the area east of Mount Lebanon, and then moved on to the Banias region where they made a comprehensive survey, photographing along the way. In preparation for a later exploration of the sources of the Jordan, they made a detailed study of the course of the river and of Lake Kinneret and surveyed Capernaum, where their finds were impressive although they made only a superficial archaeological examination. The next stops were Nazareth, the Jezreel Valley, Mount Gilboa and the hills of Samaria. In Nablus their attentions were directed to local customs and to the exploration of Mounts Gerizim and Ebal. On the way there, they were attacked by local roughs, but the Turkish authorities sent help and even offered them assistance in their work. The expedition completed its work in April 1866 after reaching Jerusalem.

The P.E.F. expedition's comprehensive report showed most of the findings to be archaeological. In Galilee remains of synagogues were uncovered, and in Bet She'an immense quantities of ancient remains were seen that awaited thorough excavation, were the means but available. Preliminary sketches were made of Bet She'an, Sebastia, Caesarea, and other places and, for the first time, Hebrew inscriptions were found in the ruins of synagogues of Nebratein and Kafr Biram. Maps of the region of the Hula Valley, the Sea of Galilee, and of Nablus were also prepared.

The scientific and administrative experience gained by the expedition was of the greatest value for the Fund's future activities — including the large-scale mapping of Western Palestine, and, at a later stage, a similar survey of Eastern Palestine. Excavations and research work were planned for Jerusalem to uncover its history; excavations of as many tels as possible, and a study of the geology, meteorology, and the natural history of the country were to round out the activities. Jerusalem, however, was to be given precedence.

# "UNDERGROUND JERUSALEM"

Lieutenant Charles **Warren**, a 27 year-old officer of the Royal Engineers, was sent in 1867 by the Palestine Exploration Fund to head its second expedition. Its aims were to continue Wilson's work in Jerusalem which had left many questions unanswered. What was the exact position of the Temple? Where were the three walls described by Josephus? Where was the City of David, Herod's palace, and the other famous sites known from classical literature? What was the true site of the Holy Sepulchre? The expedition quickly learnt of the difficulties involved in exploring Jerusalem — particularly the Temple Mount, the key to it all. The sanctity of the site made it impossible to excavate there, and so, work was begun outside the walls of the Haram enclosure. As the walls were concealed by houses and by great piles of rubble and refuse, deep rectangular shafts were sunk at some distance, and horizontal tunnels cut in the direction of the foundations of the wall. Some of the shafts were 125 feet deep.

The foundations at the south-east corner of the wall of the Temple Mount were found to be 80 feet below the surface at the time of the excavations; those at the south-west corner, 90 feet down. In the area of the north-east corner of the Haram, Warren made interesting discoveries. Adjacent to the wall here, he found a deep depression that had become filled-in in the course of the centuries, extending north-west towards Birket Isra'il. Warren thought the depression to have been part of a channel that had been constructed along the northern face of the Temple Mount.

Although Warren could not excavate within the Haram compound itself, his good relations with the guards, enabled him to make a thorough examination of the structure of the Dome of the Rock and of the network of cisterns within the area. He counted some 34 rock-hewn reservoirs of different shapes and sizes, the largest of them 43 feet deep with a capacity of over two million gallons. The next largest was 61 feet deep but held only 200,000 gallons. Warren mentions two other cisterns that are of special interest: their original purpose was not the storage of water but to serve as underground passages to the Temple compound.

199

*Wilson's Arch north of the Western Wall. (Wilson and Warren, Recovery, 1871).*

As part of his initial exploration in Jerusalem, Charles Wilson made a number of surveys of central sites in the city (in the vicinity of the Church of the Holy Sepulchre, for example). He succeeded in penetrating to underground structures and in reaching the foundations of the ancient gate to the Temple Mount. Wilson was the first to explore these remains and the ceiling, north of the Western Wall, with its imposing span, is known as Wilson's Arch to this day.

*Warren's excavations near Robinson's Arch. (Wilson and Warren, Recovery, 1871).*

Seven shafts were sunk by the Warren expedition along the Tyropoeon valley from the south-west corner of the Temple Mount wall in the direction of the Upper City to the west. The excavations showed that the bedrock at the deepest point was about 75 feet below ground level at the time. On the bottom of the valley they discovered a tunnel hewn out of rock, 12 ft. deep and 4 ft. wide. The explorers believed it to have been constructed in early times to bring water to the Lower City. Across the channel they discovered the foundations of a large pillar which apparently supported one of the arches of what they thought was a bridge carrying the street from the Upper City to the Temple compound. Remains of two collapsed arches were also found. Recent excavations at the Temple Mount have shown this supposition to be erroneous. The illustration shows the spring of the great arch first noted by Robinson, and still known by his name.

*Jews of Jerusalem. (Warren, Underground Jerusalem, 1876, p. 358).*

This photograph of Jerusalem Jews was taken by a member of Warren's expedition. Although his main interest was in historical Jerusalem, Warren's book contains a vast amount of material on the Holy City at the time of his visit.

With the growing influence of the European powers in Palestine in the fifties and sixties, the Jews secured the protection of the foreign consulates. England in particular, took a very benevolent interest in the Jewish community. This period saw a substantial growth in the number of Jews in Palestine.

Warren also began surveying beyond the present city walls. At the site of the City of David and the Ophel hill, he sank a number of shafts and came upon the remains of a wall and a tunnel — a kind of deep shaft descending from David's city to the Gihon Spring — known today as "Warren's Shaft". This may have been the very gutter, or conduit, mentioned in the Biblical account of David's conquest of Jerusalem. Another of Warren's finds was a Hebrew seal bearing the name Haggai, dating from the period of the Kingdom of Judah.

The work in Jerusalem extended from February 1867 to April 1870; and at the same time, Warren carried out surveys in other parts of the country. His reports, published in the Fund's journal, the *Quarterly Statement*, describe his tour of the Judean Desert, the shores of the Dead Sea, and Massada. He was the first European to ascend Massada from the eastern side by way of the "snake path" mentioned by Josephus, but not known to earlier explorers.

The **Palestine Exploration Fund**'s *Proceedings and Notes* of 1869 contain reports of Wilson's 1866 expedition, and of Warren's work in Jerusalem 1868—1869, together with numerous illustrations and photographs.

After Warren returned to England in 1870, the P.E.F. published, in 1871, a book he wrote jointly with Wilson, *The Recovery of Jerusalem*. In 1876, Warren summed up his work in a report entitled *Underground Jerusalem*. His next book was *The Temple or the Tomb* (1880) and, in 1884, he edited *Jerusalem*, one of the volumes of the P.E.F. report, covering all that was then known about the Holy City. It included an album of fifty plates.

Although Warren's expedition did not accomplish all it set out to do, it laid firm foundations for the topographical and historical study of ancient Jerusalem.


# SINAI — THE DESERT OF THE EXODUS

The purpose of the P.E.F.'s third expedition, in 1865, headed by Captain Wilson, was to determine whether the site of Mount Sinai — the mountain of the Giving of the Law — was Jebel Musa or Jebel Serbal, and to explore that entire region.

*Warren at Nablus — with Yakub esh-Shallaby.*
*(Palestine Exploration Fund photograph).*

After excavating in Jerusalem, Warren made a journey to Philistia in May 1867, visiting Gaza and Ashkelon. Here he mapped an area of 800 square miles, making numerous altitude measurements. He also travelled in the Judean Desert, the Jordan Valley, Transjordan, and the Lebanon, gathering new and valuable information on ancient sites, ruins, and temples. On one of his journeys he visited Shekhem (Nablus) where he met Yakub esh-Shallaby, the head of the Samaritan community.

204

*Members of the Sinai Survey — 1868-9. (Palestine Exploration Fund photograph).*

The Palestine Exploration Fund ordnance survey expedition to Sinai under Wilson and H.S. Palmer included such well-known members as the Reverend Holland (honorary secretary of the Fund), Prof. E.H. Palmer, Mr Wyatt the naturalist, and four officers of the Royal Engineers. The survey took six months, during which time an area of about 4,000 square miles was mapped. The area included Jebel Musa and Jebel Sirbal as well as the strip along the presumed route taken by the Children of Israel between Egypt and the traditional mountain of the Giving of the Law. The expedition reached the conclusion that Jebel Musa and not Sirbal was the Biblical Mount Sinai. In the photograph, from right to left, are Wyatt, Holland, Wilson, H.S. Palmer, E.H. Palmer, and two Bedouin guides, Salem and Hassan.

A summary of the expedition's activities, by Frederick Holland, one of its members, was included in Wilson and Warren's *The Recovery of Jerusalem*. A full report of the Sinai Survey by C. **Wilson** and H.S. **Palmer**, was published by the Ordnance Survey in 1869. Each of the three volumes — From Suez to Mt. Sinai (Jebel Musa), Wadi Feiran and Mt. Serbal, and Sinaitic and Egyptian inscriptions contains illustrations, maps, plans, and cross-sections of the regions surveyed.

Since Wilson's party had covered the area between Egypt and Jebel Musa but not the northern and eastern parts of the Sinai Peninsula, the Palestine Exploration Fund commissioned a further expedition to cover those regions. The new team consisted of Professor Edward **Palmer** and Tyrwhitt **Drake** who on behalf of Cambridge University was to examine the natural history of these areas. Twelve days after leaving Suez they reached Jebel Musa; from there they went on to Ein Hudera — the most easterly point of the previous survey, and on to the Muslim pilgrim road to Nakhl; they traversed the upper reaches of Wadi El-Arish to Jebel Araif en-Na'aqa and visited the supposed site of Qadesh Barnea. Thence, they made their way to Beersheba and Jerusalem, returning south some months later to explore part of the Negev mountain plateau. From what they saw of the Bedouin way of life in Northern Sinai and in the Negev, Palmer thought that to call these people the sons of the desert was a misnomer; they should more properly be considered fathers of the desert, for much of the desert was due to their destructive ways.

In Jerusalem, Palmer interested himself in the history of the Dome of the Rock and, on a tiled decorative band around the inside of the dome, found the date of the mosque's construction, 72 of the Hejira — 691 C.E. Palmer's discovery confirmed that the shrine was built by the Ommayad caliph, Abd el-Melek, and not by the Abbasid caliph Abdullah Mamoun who renovated the structure in the year 831 C.E. and changed the inscription to claim credit for himself as the original builder — forgetting only to have the original date erased!

The account of Palmer and Drake's journey was published in the Palestine Exploration Fund's *Quarterly Statement* in 1871, and appeared in greater detail, later that year, in Palmer's book *The Desert of the Exodus*.

Despite the valuable information brought back by these explorers, it was evident that a more complete survey of the Negev was needed — but that had to wait until 1913. Tyrwhitt Drake continued studying other parts

*The Orientalist, E.H. Palmer. (Palestine Exploration Fund photograph).*

As Professor Palmer became familiar with the Bedouin on his first journey to Sinai and the Negev, he was asked in 1882 to persuade the sheikhs to remain neutral during the British occupation of Egypt. He made his way from Gaza to Sinai where he met with the principal sheikhs, and reached Suez after having successfully completed his mission. Later, he was again asked to visit the Bedouin. This time Palmer carried a large sum in gold coin to pay off the tribesmen and was accompanied by two British officers, a servant, and a Jewish cook from Jaffa. After leaving Ayun Musa on 8 August they reached Wadi Suder, where they were murdered by Bedouin. Warren was sent out to search for the bodies and found their remains in a wadi.

207

*Gate at El-'Abdeh (Avdat—Eboda) — 1870. (Palmer and Drake, 1871, II, p. 410).*

Prof. Palmer and Tyrwhitt Drake were members of the Sinai Ordnance Survey expedition of 1868. After the survey they travelled through the northern parts of Sinai, entering the Negev by way of the Kadesh Barnea region. Investigating the ruins of several Byzantine cities, they noted the existence of ancient reservoirs, irrigation channels, agricultural terraces (near Aujah-Nitzana), and small mounds of stones, which the Arabs called "mounds of grapes", and which the explorers believed to be remains of some kind of irrigation system attesting the cultivation of vines in the desert. Palmer and Drake investigated the antiquities of Nitzana, Esbeita (Shivta) and Khalasa (Halutza), and on a second journey from Hebron to the Arava and Mount Hor, correctly identified the ruins of ancient Abda (Avdat). They visited Petra and reached Moab via the Dead Sea, from where they returned to Jerusalem by way of Dhiban and Jericho. The above illustration was prepared from one of Tyrwhitt Drake's photographs and appeared in Palmer's book *The Desert of the Exodus.*

208

of Palestine and the neighbouring areas — especially Northern Syria — and also participated in the P.E.F. mapping survey.

S.C. **Bartlett,** in 1873—4, followed part of Palmer and Drake's route in the desert and attempted to deal also with the question of the geography of the Exodus. The book he published has beautiful illustrations, some of them reproduced from Palmer and Drake. The geologist Oscar **Fraas** made a valuable contribution to the study of the rock structure of Sinai and Palestine. Richard **Burton,** regarded as one of the most important explorers of Syria, wrote *Unexplored Syria,* together with Drake, but the work contains almost no material on Palestine. Burton's wife, Isabel, on the other hand, put her experiences and observations on paper for the edification of ladies interested in the life of women in the Holy Land. Her *Inner Life of Syria, Palestine, and the Holy Land, from a Private Journal,* illustrates folk ways and domestic practices. Other women travellers who published their impressions were a Miss **Kraft** from America and Lady **Herbert** from England.

The greatest find of those years was that of F.A. **Klein,** a French priest from Alsace, who in 1868, near the Arnon gorge in Transjordan, discovered a black basalt stele one metre high and some sixty centimetres wide with an inscription in ancient Hebrew by Mesha, King of Moab. The discovery caused a sensation in the world of learning and gave an impetus to the further investigation of the Holy Land's past.

In the second half of the 19th century, an ever-growing number of pocket guide-books on the Holy Land appeared on the bookstalls to meet the needs of tourists and pilgrims. Written from various points of view — religious and secular — these little vademecums constitute an important record of the changes, from year to year, of the sites accessible to visitors and of the social and economic state of the country. The names of their authors and publishers — **Baedeker,** Thomas **Cook, MacMillan,** Father **Liévin** de Hamme, etc. — soon became part of every tourist's vocabulary.

# THE GREAT SURVEY OF WESTERN PALESTINE

Surveying and mapping Western Palestine was the main aim of the Palestine Exploration Fund. After the initial success of the Jerusalem expeditions, it was decided to undertake this massive project, and to entrust it to the Royal Engineers. A first party set out in 1871, under the auspices of the Society and the War Office.

At first, the party was headed by Captain Stewart and, when malaria compelled him to return to England, Tyrwhitt Drake, the expedition's Arabic interpreter and expert on archaeology and natural history took his place. After some 560 square miles had been surveyed and charted, Lieutenant Claude Conder took over. Throughout the course of the work, Drake and Conder submitted regular reports to the Fund's *Quarterly Statement*.

In the first two years, the area between the coast to the West, and from Nazareth to the North, and Jerusalem to the South, was mapped. In the autumn of 1873 the survey of Philistia and Judea was begun, and in November of that year the survey teams descended to the Jordan Valley and Jericho, where, owing to fever, work was suspended. All along, trouble was encountered from the local inhabitants who destroyed triangulation points, believing treasure to be hidden underneath. Work was resumed in February 1874, at Lake Kinneret. In May 1874, Conder returned to England to report personally on the progress made. While he was away, Drake died of fever in Jerusalem; being replaced by a 24-year-old lieutenant of the Royal Engineers who was destined to gain world fame as Lord Kitchener of Khartoum and Secretary for War during World War I. The survey continued until June 1875, when the expedition was attacked by Arabs at Safed. Work was again halted and only resumed early in 1877 after the case had been heard in the Akko law court. At the time, Conder and Kitchener were both in London and the resumption of the project was now assigned to the latter, while Conder set about preparing the material for publication.

By September 1877, the mapping of Western Palestine was virtually completed. The survey covered an area of some 6,000 square miles, from Tyre to Banias in the North, and from Gaza to Be'er Sheva in the South.

The three volumes of the report accompanied a map in twenty-six sheets, with a chapter of text to each sheet going into great detail of the landscape, topography, agricultural utilization, hydrography, points of habitation listed alphabetically and according to administrative districts, population, roads, historical sites, religions, and the flora and fauna.

There are faults in the report. Villages are not uniformly described, since this was done by different field workers, and the categorization of local populations by race and religion relied upon untested information. On the other hand, water resources, roads, archaeological sites — many of which have since disappeared — religious buildings and folk customs are dealt with comprehensively and in detail. As an example of the thoroughness of the work, the maps give the Arabic names of some 9,000 villages, ruins, mountains, rivers, and springs as compared with only about 1,800 such place names in Van de Velde's map.

The country had now been systematically covered for the first time. The report formed the basis for all later exploration of Palestine, especially of subsequent mapping.

A distinguished literary figure, Walter **Besant**, Honorary Secretary of the Palestine Exploration Fund, was the moving spirit behind the expeditions. In 1871, he and Edward **Palmer**, wrote *Jerusalem, the City of Herod and Saladin* which went into numerous editions. He also wrote histories of the Fund's work — *Twenty-One Years' Work in the Holy Land* (1886), and *Thirty Years' Work in the Holy Land* (1895), as well as the biography of his friend, Edward Henry Palmer who had been murdered by Bedouins in Sinai in 1882 at the time of the British occupation of Egypt. A review of 50 years of P.E.F. activity in the Holy Land was written in 1915 by Colonel Watson.

George **Armstrong**, who followed Besant as secretary of the Fund, had been a member of the Palestine survey team and participated in a later expedition to survey the Arava. He has to his credit the construction of relief maps of Palestine made on the basis of the P.E.F. surveys.

In 1890, the P.E.F. maps were reissued to a scale of 3/8 inch to 1 mile, giving modern place-names for both sides of the Jordan, as well as Old and New Testament place-names. There were two editions — one in 20 sheets, the other in 12. Three years later a relief map was made to the same scale, and in 1902 a smaller one of 1 inch: 5 miles. Armstrong also wrote a treatise, *Names and Places in the Old and New Testament and their Modern Identification.*

*Kitchener, as a young man. (Palestine Exploration Fund photograph).*

Kitchener's contribution to the exploration of the Palestine is merely a sub-chapter in a dazzling career. Lord Kitchener rose from Lieutenant to Field Marshal in the British army. He was a hero of the war in the Sudan, Sirdar of Egypt, and was appointed Secretary for War in 1914. In 1916 when on a mission to Russia, then Britain's ally in the war, his ship struck a mine and he went down with it. Kitchener's writings on Palestine consist mainly of reports to the *PEF*; some of them describe early synagogues in Galilee, a number of which he discovered and investigated. His main work in Palestine was the surveying and mapping of the North and the Arava.

212

*Conrad Schick (Palestine Exploration Fund photograph).*

The Swiss architect Conrad Schick, was a resident of Jerusalem since 1846. He started his explorations in Palestine at about the same time the PEF began its work there. Most of his writings, however, were only published later. His architectural knowledge of Jerusalem was of great help, particularly to Charles Wilson, with whom he co-operated. Schick determined the bedrock level in all places that were being examined, thus making it possible to reconstruct the original topography of the site on which the Holy City was built. He continued surveying Jerusalem until his death in 1901. The results of his work were published in the journals of the British and German societies, but later (1887, 1896) he wrote books on the Temple and the Temple Mount area.

213

*Ruins of church, Kuryet El Enab. (Abu Ghosh).*
*(Conder and Kitchener, SWP Memoirs, 1883, III, p. 132).*

The PEF's general report, *The Survey of Western Palestine*, which appeared in seven large volumes, contained the following sections.

1. The *Jerusalem* volume, giving a complete account of the excavations by Captain Warren, together with a description of other researches in the Holy City by Captain Wilson, Lieutenant Conder, Clermont-Ganneau, Dr. Chaplin, Dr. Schick and others.

2. *The Name Lists*, containing more than 10,000 names collected during the survey, transliterated and translated by Lieutenant Conder and edited by Professor Palmer.

3. *The Special Papers*, being a reproduction of papers which had already appeared in the *Quarterly Statement*.

4. *The Flora and Fauna of Palestine*, by the Rev. Canon Tristram.

5. *The Memoirs*, in three volumes, containing the drawings, plans, sketches and notes made by the survey officers, supplemented by such other information as could be obtained from authentic sources.

The above illustration is an example of the pictures included in the expedition's memoirs.

*Nebi Samwil. (Conder and Kitchener, SWP Memoirs, 1883, III, p. 152).*

The instructions of the P.E.F. expedition were to plot important places; to make detailed plans of ancient buildings, ruins, graves, and the like; to take photographs; collect artifacts and geological specimens; to collect samples of animals and plants, and to photograph inscriptions and architectural details. The picture of Nebi Samwil is a good example of their work.

Two years after the completion of the Palestine Exploration Fund Survey of Western Palestine, a detailed map was published, in 26 large sheets, to a scale of one inch to the mile (1:63,360). Two years later, a smaller edition appeared (six sheets, scale 3/8 inch to the mile) in four separate forms: with Arabic names, with Old Testament place-names, with New Testament place-names, and showing the drainage basins of rivers and streams.

*Samaritan place of sacrifice, Mount Gerizim — (Shortly before Passover).*
*(Conder and Kitchener, SWP Memoirs, 1882, II, p. 188).*

In the 19th century, the Samaritans lived in the south-western section of Nablus. According to a census in 1874, the community consisted of 135 individuals, including 28 married couples, 10 elderly widows, 49 young bachelors and 20 unmarried girls. The community obviously suffered from a lack of women! A number of writers noted that the numbers steadily diminished in the course of the century. Visitors always showed particular interest in the Samaritan synagogue, the scrolls of the Law, and the place of sacrifice on Mt. Gerizim.

*Camp of Lortet's expedition. (Lortet, 1884, p. 217).*

In the second half of the seventies, a French biological expedition under Lortet visited Syria and Palestine. Their report contains numerous excellent illustrations engraved after photographs. The caption to the above picture reads "Notre Campement sous le pin de Godefroy de Bouillon". The large Aleppo pine still stands opposite the north wall of the Old City of Jerusalem.

*Explorers at rest. (Palestine Exploration Fund photograph 1883).*

The Arava, stretching from the Dead Sea in the north to the Gulf of Aqaba (Elat) in the south, remained largely unknown even after the completion of the Western Palestine survey. The object of the expedition to the Arava, under Prof. Hull, was to explore and map the region. Kitchener was in charge of the mapping, with Armstrong as his assistant.

The expedition set out from Egypt for Mount Sinai in the winter of 1883. Then, from the Aqaba shore, they moved north along the Arava to the Dead Sea. After completing the survey, the expedition continued to Beer Sheba and Gaza. At Tel Abu Hureira, south of Gaza, Kitchener left the party and returned to Egypt. The others went on from Gaza to Jaffa and Jerusalem and descended again to the Dead Sea.

218

# FILLING IN THE GAPS: THE ARAVA, TRANSJORDAN AND THE NEGEV

The P.E.F. survey was rounded out with the mapping of the Negev and the Arava, and research in Transjordan.

In 1883, an expedition was sent out to the Arava. It was headed by E. **Hull**, a geologist, with Kitchener in charge of mapping of the area between Mount Sinai and the Arava Valley, bounded by the Tih Plateau to the west and the mountains of Edom to the east. Hull produced two books on this work. The first, in 1885, was *Mount Seir, Sinai and Western Palestine*, with much excellent material on the Arava and good illustrations and maps — including a geological map. Hull's second book, *The Geology of Palestine and Arabia Petraea* gives a detailed description of his findings, which, though outdated now, and largely incorrect, represented a considerable achievement in his day. A later book, published in 1910, deals with personal reminiscences of his work in Palestine.

The mapping of the Negev, south of the Gaza—Be'er Sheva line up to the Egyptian border running from Rafa to the head of the Gulf of Elat, was undertaken in 1913 by Captain S.F. Newcombe and Lieutenant F.C.S. Greig. C.L. **Woolley** and T.E. Lawrence, both to become famous for other activities in the Near East, joined his team for a few weeks. During their brief stay in the area, Woolley and Lawrence explored sites that showed signs of having once been inhabited. They investigated and sketched the ruins of the Negev's ancient cities, studying the methods by which the meagre rainfall of the desert had been utilized to irrigate crops and fruit trees. Across the border, in Sinai, they explored Qosseima, and identified En Qudeirat as the Biblical Qadesh Barnea. The results of their investigations were published in the *P.E.F. Annual* of 1914—1915 under the title *The Wilderness of Zin*. Newcombe's map of the Negev was kept as a military secret and only released after World War I.

The research and mapping of Transjordan was the first project of the **American Palestine Exploration Society** (A.P.E.S.), established in 1870 in the wake of the P.E.F. But the Society was disbanded in 1884 without carrying out this project. Two preliminary expeditions however, were sent out under its auspices, one under Lieutenant Steever in 1873, the other under Lane. The second expedition, included as archaeologist and head of research, Dr. Selah **Merill**, later to become American consul in Jerusalem. In 1881, Merill brought out the book *East of the Jordan*, containing two reports on the work done in 1875 and 1877. In the same year he also wrote *Galilee in the Time of Christ*, and, in 1908, *Ancient Jerusalem*.

The American society having failed, the P.E.F. decided to complete the mapping of the Holy Land east of Jordan. In 1881, a small contingent under Captain C.R. **Conder** began surveying the southern part of Gilead and the north of Moab — the area of the El Adwan Bedouins, one of the largest tribes in Transjordan. The Turkish governor, however, was suspicious, hindered their work, and finally prohibited it altogether despite great efforts on their behalf by the British ambassador in Constantinople. But by then, the expedition had managed to survey an area of 500 square miles. The results are given by Conder in one of the P.E.F. reports, *The Survey of Eastern Palestine*, and in his book, *Heth and Moab*. Conder turned out to be one of the most important explorers of Palestine and an incredibly prolific writer and editor. Röhricht's bibliography devotes six full pages to the listing of Conder's work, citing 143 items — and that only until 1890.

What the British and American societies were unable to carry out, was completed by one man, the German engineer Gottlieb **Schumacher**, a resident of Haifa. For twenty years Schumacher was engaged in the mapping of Transjordan, sometimes on behalf of the German Society for the Exploration of Palestine, sometimes for the P.E.F., but mostly while working for the Turkish railways as a survey engineer.

His house in the Haifa Templar colony was a haven for the Fund's explorers during their survey of the north of the country, but long before that Schumacher had been interested in the Holy Land and its historic past. Part of his work for the Turks entailed a survey along the Damascus-Haifa railway line, particularly the Edrei (Dera'a) — Samakh branch, which he combined with the mapping of Transjordan. The German and British exploration societies assisted him with his publications. His first book, *Across the Jordan* (1886), contained the first maps of certain parts of Transjordan. His next books *The Jaulan* (1888) and *Abila, Pella and the Northern Ajlun* (1889), also had new maps, this time of the northern part of Gilead.

Schumacher drew his maps to the scale and format of those of the P.E.F.

and they therefore complement and continue the latter; they are just as detailed and constitute no less an achievement.

A number of his writings appeared in the journals of the British and German societies; one notable article, in the P.E.F. *Quarterly Statement* of 1887, gives his estimates of the population of the Akko district according to its various groupings.

The Deutsche Verein zur Erforschung Palästinas was established in 1877 on much the same lines as the P.E.F. German explorers understood that their work would be easier if they had the support of an organized body with an adequate budget. By 1870 the German consulate was firmly entrenched in Jerusalem. German visitors were arriving in increasing numbers, among them explorers who did not wish to rely on any foreign institution for their publications, and who wished to have funds granted for protracted stays in the country and for local labour crews. The new German association met these needs.

In 1878, the first issue of the Association's journal *Zeitschrift des deutschen Palästina Vereins* was published, edited by H. Guthe of Leipzig, a future participant in excavations in Jerusalem. The Association's first project was the exploration of Transjordan, the resulting maps being based on the work of Schumacher. The focus soon shifted to archaeological research, with a series of excavations in Jerusalem and elsewhere in the country.

The exploration of Transjordan in the eighties, particularly in the Gilead region, dovetailed to some extent with the activities of Laurence **Oliphant**, who initiated plans for Jewish settlement in Palestine. In 1870, this eccentric of Scot origins, set out to investigate the prospects for the realization of such a project in the hope of obtaining Turkish agreement to his settlement plans. The results of his journey appear in his *The Land of Gilead*, a book full of interesting details about various regions of Palestine and setting forth his ideas on Jewish settlement.

Oliphant who resided in the Druse village of Daliyat el-Carmel also published a collection of fascinating letters entitled *Haifa, or Life in Modern Palestine* 1882, providing deep insights into current affairs and out of the way places — mainly in Galilee.

Individual explorers continued, despite limited resources, to add

*Captured on the Jordan by Arabs of the Hooleh. (Hulah).*
*(MacGregor, 1870. Frontispiece).*

John MacGregor, who visited Palestine in 1868—69, was one of the most daring travellers of his time. An experienced navigator, he had sailed many rivers in many countries and the tales of his adventures made him a popular figure. A good Christian, he wished to combine his favourite occupation with a visit to the Holy Land. The most interesting and best-known part of his journey was his canoe cruise in the marshes of the Hulah Valley and the lake, the upper reaches of the Jordan and the Sea of Galilee (Lake Kinneret). On the Hulah he was taken prisoner by the wild swamp-dwelling Bedouin.

222

*Hooleh (Hulah) huts. (MacGregor, 1870, p. 235).*

Mac Gregor's *Rob Roy on the Jordan* was one of the most popular books on the Holy Land. "Rob Roy" was the name of the canoe on which he planned to move down the length of the Jordan, as Costigan, Molyneux and Lynch had done before him, but obstacles along the river from a point south of Lake Kinneret, compelled MacGregor to return. From his description and maps of the Hulah Valley the observer may discern the changes that have taken place in the region today. MacGregor enjoyed considerable assistance from the PEF, which placed at his disposal original material such as the maps of the Wilson-Anderson expedition (See p. 198). His personal diary, today in the PEF library in London, includes his notes and measurements.

considerably to the knowledge of the country and helped in the unveiling of its secrets.

One of the most distinguished of these was the Frenchman, Charles **Clermont-Ganneau**, secretary at the French consulate in Jerusalem. Clermont-Ganneau carried out researches in conjunction with the P.E.F. in 1873 and 1874 as well as independent archaeological surveys in Jerusalem, in the Jaffa region southwards to Gaza, and in Samaria. Apart from a number of works in French on Palestine, the Fund published his findings and writings, at first in the *Quarterly Statement*, and in 1896 and 1899, in two large volumes, *Archaeological Researches*.

Among the many travellers and explorers of this period are Samuel **Manning** who was in Palestine in 1873. His attractive book *Those Holy Fields, Palestine illustrated by pen and pencil*, published by the London Religious Tract Society is profusely illustrated with pictures, both original and some taken from recent publications, including those of the P.E.F. Other important works are those of Nepomuk **Sepp** and C. von **Orelli**, professor of Bible at Basle University, whose travel diary based on the letters he wrote during February-March 1876 includes new information. The Reverend James **Neil**, resident in Jerusalem between 1871 and 1874, left three books on the Holy Land to posterity: *Palestine Repeopled*, *Palestine Explored*, and *Pictured Palestine*. Some of the illustrations in Neil's books were by Henry **Harper** who also himself published several illustrated volumes.

Jewish writings too, began to proliferate in the seventies reflecting the development of Jewish settlement in Palestine, the establishment of new suburbs outside the walls of Jerusalem, and the various attempts by Jews to settle on the land.

The clergyman John Cunningham **Geikie**, who visited Palestine several times, showed particular interest in Conder's archaeological work. He was the author of a number of popular books on Biblical and religious themes. Like many other authors on the subject, Geikie prefaces his extremely popular *The Holy Land and the Bible*, first published in 1887, with a justification for placing yet another book on Palestine on the market. His purpose, he explains, is to provide the student of the Bible with illustrations of the landscape settings to the Scriptures and to the manners and customs of the people of the land of the Bible that have changed only very little over the millennia. And indeed, his work is crammed with drawings and engravings of photographs. The frequent re-editions bear out Geikie's contention that such a volume answered a decided need of the Bible-reading public.

Charles **Wilson**'s elegant four-volume compendium *Picturesque Palestine, Sinai and Egypt*, which appeared in 1880, was the product of co-operation between him and the greatest of the contemporary Palestine explorers.

The following contributed to the first volume, Introduction — Stanley; Jerusalem — Wilson himself; Bethlehem and North Judea — Tristram; the Judean Mountains and Ephraim — Conder; Samaria and the Jezreel Valley — Miss M.E. Rogers; the Jezreel Valley and Nazareth — Tristram; Galilee — Merill; Northern Galilee, Caesarea and the Galilee Mountains — Merill. Certain parts of Syria, too, such as the Hermon, Damascus, Palmyra and Baalbek are covered in this volume as well. Phoenicia and Lebanon are the first subjects of the second volume, followed by Akko, the Carmel and the coastal towns, described by Miss Rogers; Lod, Ramla and Philistia — Warren; Southern Judea — Tristram; the Judean Desert and the Dead Sea — E.H. Palmer. The final chapters review Edom, Sinai, the St. Catherin Monastery and various parts of Egypt. Hundreds of drawings, some 300 woodcuts and 20 steel engravings, mostly after photographs, illustrate these fine volumes.

In 1883, the German explorers Guthe and Ebers published Wilson's work in German, including most of the illustrations. Many of Wilson's pictures also appear in the German version of one of Guérin's books — *Das heil. Land.*

In general, Wilson affords the reader an overall pictorial survey of Palestine. The pictures are artistic compositions, but never at the expense of true representation, and admirably convey both the spirit of the times and the state of hundreds of sites in the Holy Land and the surrounding regions.

Although his work falls outside the time limit of this survey, no account of the development of the geographical research of Palestine would be complete without mention of one whose name is inseparably linked with the concept of the historical geography of the Holy Land.

George Adam Smith was professor of Hebrew and Old Testament Exegesis at Glasgow and Aberdeen, and also studied Arabic. His first journey through Palestine, in 1880, was made mostly on foot: he returned again in

225

1899, 1901, and 1904. His famous *The Historical Geography of the Holy Land* was written after his first journey. Among his other books particular mention must be made of *Jerusalem* and his *Historical Atlas of the Holy Land*, first published in 1914.

The *Historical Geography of the Holy Land* has become a classic for both experts and students of the subject, but also for the general reader. The penetrating observations and analyses, and the beauty of its language makes it a work of art in itself: its popularity and timelessness is attested by a 26th edition being published in 1966.

In the introduction to the first edition, George Adam Smith explains that his purpose is to depict the general aspect of Palestine so that the scholar might feel his pulse throb when in the country. The Biblical student, he states, must acquire a comprehensive knowledge of the physical structure, appearance, and sites of the country, which will make it possible for him to understand its historical development. This follows the deterministic thinking prevalent at that time. The book itself, however, does not state this explicitly. Smith leaves it for his vivid description of the country's character to suggest the possible influences of physical structure on the history of Palestine, in Biblical and other periods.

George Adam Smith's revelation of the geography of this ancient land to a new and progress-conscious world might be taken as a fitting conclusion to this review of the geographical-historical sources for the study of 19th century Palestine.

*Abraham's Oak, Hebron. (Wilson, Picturesque Palestine, 1880, III, p. 193).*

Hundreds of woodcuts and steel engravings of photographs appear in Wilson's book *Picturesque Palestine, Sinai and Egypt.* The pictures were made from original sketches and form a valuable record of plant life in Palestine, Syria, and Egypt at the end of the 19th century. This illustration is of the oak tree near Hebron, traditionally called "Abraham's Oak". "One of the lower branches was broken down by a heavy fall of snow in the winter of 1850. It was cut up into logs and conveyed to Jerusalem; there were seven camel-loads; one log was sent to England".

*Safed. The Jewish Quarter (Wilson, Picturesque Palestine, 1880, II, p. 90).*

At the beginning of the 19th century, the population of Safed was 6,000—7,000, of which a third to half were Jews. The earthquake in 1837 caused great devastation and many deaths in the Jewish Quarter. However, the tow was quickly rebuilt. More Jews came, as well as Arabs from Morocco, and within a short time the population had regained its numbers. The illustration shows part of the Jewish section on the northwest side of the hill immediately below the fortress.

228

# EPILOGUE

The last twenty years of the nineteenth century saw the inception of organised Zionist settlement in the Land of Israel. Travellers and explorers from the West continued coming to the country, and the fashion of writing books of travel and discovery kept up right to the end of the Ottoman Empire — and after it — so long as Palestine remained a land of mystery and Oriental character with regions difficult of access. But during the last four decades of Ottoman rule, Zionist settlement became the dominant factor influencing the landscape and the history of the country. The study of the country must therefore switch its focus from discovery and research to this new phenomenon.

How would the landscape of Palestine have fared in the absence of the Zionist factor? To imagine such a situation today is difficult. It is very likely that some measure of modernization would have continued to penetrate and shape the character of the country. But as we try to fill in our imaginary picture, the questions will arise: Would Palestine have undergone a development similar to the other lands of the Middle East? Would the country have remained unique because of its sanctity to Christians and Jews in Jerusalem and the other holy cities — Bethlehem, Nazareth, Hebron, Tiberias, Safed, etc.? Would the character of the country have remained similar to what it had been in mid-nineteenth century, or would it have been influenced and changed by the new technologies in agriculture, industry, commerce, urbanisation, etc.? To build up such an image today is no more than idle speculation — for along came the Zionist movement and provided its own dynamic.

At the end of four centuries of Ottoman rule in Palestine, Zionist activities were still relegated almost exclusively to agricultural settlement. It is true that at the same time urban development went on as well — but this had hardly any connection with Zionist ideology. Thus for example, new neighbourhoods — some of these non-Jewish — rose outside the walls of Jerusalem: overcrowded conditions in the Old City drove many of the inhabitants to erect housing projects outside, but these usually maintained their closed community character. The same process went on in other urban centers as well. In Haifa, the expansion of the town and the port were spurred by the German Templars, by the connection of the railway to the Hedjaz line, and by the construction of large flour mills by the Turkish authorities. The Ottoman government also planned and constructed roads and railways, especially to serve its needs during World War I. None of this was motivated by the Zionist movement. In fact, the new Jewish suburb of Jaffa — Tel Aviv, the major project of renewed Jewish settlement in the country, was only founded in 1910, on the eve of the war, and was abandoned and destroyed during the hostilities. The beginning of large-scale Zionist settlement must therefore be sought in the Mandatory period. This true of the first properly-planned Jewish urban neighbourhoods: Rehavia and Bet ha-Kerem in Jerusalem, Hadar and Mount Carmel in Haifa, and Kiryat Shemu'el in Tiberias — all these date to the early years of the British Mandate in Palestine.

Thus, at the end of the Ottoman period, Zionist influence was felt mainly in the realm of rural settlement. At that time the seeds for renewed Jewish life were sown, but in the years before British troops conquered the land, little had germinated to seriously affect the landscape of the country. For example, a comparison of the impact made by the German Templar colonies and by Turkish development projects with that of the early Zionist settlements show that the latter were almost insignificant factors in the landscape. The picture is, of course, totally different if the overall period, from the beginning of the 20th century to our own day is considered. Where are the German Templars, whose influence was so great a century ago? It is Zionist settlement that had an overwhelming effect on shaping the present face of the country. Any systematic study of events in the latter years of Ottoman rule in Palestine, from a point of view of historical geography, must give prime consideration to the early stages of Zionist settlement to understand subsequent developments.

The present survey does not extend to these matters, restricting itself to the first eighty years of the 19th century, up to the eve of organised Zionist settlement. These eight decades may well be considered the 'Age of Rediscovery' of the Holy Land.

This ancient land never ceased to interest and occupy the thoughts of the Western world. Long before modern scientific research began to unravel its secrets and hidden places, people wanted to find out about the Holy Land. Those who came to do so in the last century were keenly aware of the pioneering character of their researches and work. Like other explorers who penetrated unknown regions, these early nineteenth

230

century travellers probed their way into regions Western man had not set foot in for hundreds of years. They sought out places of which only the names were remembered from sacred or classical literature, but whose physical existence was buried under the dust of ages. In this wasteland, courageous explorers succeeded in laying the foundations of scientific research. Their journeys to gather information and advance the study of Palestine were subject to incessant adventure and danger to life and limb. The explorations of Seetzen and Burckhardt, Robinson and Lynch, van de Velde and Tristram, and the officers of the Palestine Exploration Fund, easily hold their own in comparison with those of the best-known travellers of the age. The Palestine explorers prepared to meet any eventuality; their successes were often due to sheer pluck and daring improvisation to save their skins while keeping unflinchingly to their demanding, self-imposed tasks. They dissimulated their true identity and purpose in hostile surroundings, learned the languages and ways of a fanatical native population, invented tales, and conjured up pretexts to explain their suspicious behaviour to those who would impede their progress. Not all of these intrepid travellers reached home safely. Costigan, Molyneux, Lieutenant Dale of the Lynch expedition, Tyrwhitt Drake, and Edward Palmer — and others as well — paid with their lives for their contribution to the exploration of the country.

Among those who participated in the rediscovery of the Holy Land were some of the leading personalities of the times: writers and poets, artists and statesmen, clergymen and army officers, research workers in many fields, and scientists. Many of those who came, regarded the rediscovery of the Holy Land as part of the exploration of the Middle East — or the Levant, as it was called then — incorporating Palestine in comprehensive itineraries through the countries of the East. The exploration of Palestine, therefore, may be considered a stage in this wider context which included the spectacular archaeological discoveries in Mesopotamia and Egypt, in Asia Minor, the Greek Islands, and even in the Arabian Peninsula.

In several newly-opened regions of the world, the age of exploration heralded the inception of modern European colonialism. Similar aims are often attributed to the powers when tracing the history of imperialism in the Middle East before World War I. And indeed, among the explorers and survey teams working in the Holy Land there were undoubtedly some who carried out imperialist missions and whose scientific work was not their sole preoccupation in the country. But, everything considered, it becomes clear that power politics played a surprisingly minor role — at least as regards the exploration of Palestine. Most explorers were motivated purely by the drive to engage in true scientific research and to uncover the secrets of the Holy Land.

In many parts of the world, the age of exploration was a harbinger of colonization: in the wake of the explorers came settlers. Western man was presented with new prospects of conquering virgin territories with untold effects upon the fate of both the old and the new lands. This was not true of the Middle East for its rediscovery had no perceptible effect on its basic condition. There are several explanations for this. First, the study of these ancient lands aimed exclusively at uncovering their past history and at discovering the centers of ancient cultures forgotten over the ages. Then too, explorers in the Levant did not come upon new countries or unpopulated regions rich in fertile soil and natural resources that stirred Europeans to settlement and exploitation. Nor were the local inhabitants of particular interest to the travellers — at least not to the extent of arousing a desire for socially or economically advantageous contacts with them. The activities of Europeans in the countries of the Levant therefore did not follow the colonial pattern of the period, and very little change occurred in the rural landscape.

Is there any connection between the spectacular advance in the basic exploration and rediscovery of the ancient Land of Israel and the beginnings of Zionist settlement of Jews in their historic homeland? As may be seen from this survey, the great majority of explorers and travellers were not Jews, while the concerns of the early Zionist settlers — and of the movement as a whole — were far removed from the scientific study of the country. Only after Jewish settlement became more firmly rooted, did Jews gradually begin to take part in the exploration of their country and to replace foreigners in all aspects of Palestine research. In the foregoing pages a few Jewish travellers are mentioned, but they played only a very minor role. One of the most important among them, Rabbi Joseph Schwarz — whom we have singled-out as the first Jewish geographer of modern times — even took his compatriots to task for not engaging in the "sacred knowledge of the Land". This deficiency was elevated to a virtue by one of the spiritual fathers of the first efforts at Zionist immigration and settlement in Palestine, Rabbi Yehiel Michal Piness, who stated emphatically that he had no interest in the researches of the wise men from among the Gentiles. While making practical use of their maps, he rejected their opinions and theories. The exploration of the Land of Israel was thus as far removed from the consciousness of the Jewish settlers of 19th century Palestine as it was from the concerns of Jews elsewhere. Unlike colonization movements in newly-explored parts of the world, Jewish-Zionist settlement in Palestine was not the result of material inducements such as rich land, cheap labour, or the exploitation of natural resources. On the contrary, despite the country's poverty and neglect, Jews came to it — for idealistic reasons — to reclaim their ancient land and restore it to its former fruitfulness.

At most, the rediscovery of Palestine and the beginning of modern Jewish settlement there were indirectly connected. Both thrived on the decline of the Ottoman Empire and the growing influence of the West. But the two processes were really unrelated, occurring at about the same time but each proceeding from its own logic. The rediscovery of the Land of Israel was well under way when the people of Israel began to rediscover their ancient homeland. The first pioneers of Jewish settlement in the country laid the foundations of renewed Jewish life as the first stage in the geographical rediscovery of the country comes to an end.

# BIBLIOGRAPHY

## A. PRIMARY SOURCES

The following books, articles, maps and views were consulted in the preparation of this survey. The number at the end of each entry, in brackets, refers to the serial numbers in Reinhold Röhricht's *Bibliotheca Geographica Palaestinae* (2nd. ed.) Jerusalem 1963. Röhricht's bibliography provides additional details on the work mentioned and lists other books and articles by the same author. Works not listed by Röhricht, or those published after 1878 have no reference number. The year, in parentheses, after the author's name, indicates the time of the visit to the country as given by Röhricht.

Many of the titles listed here, appeared in a number of editions and formats.

Addison, C.G. (1838). *Damascus and Palmyra: a Journey to the East. With a Sketch of the State ... under Ibrahim Pasha.* London 1838. 2 vols. [1870].

Alderson, R.C. (1841). "Notes on Acre". *Papers on Subjects Connected with the Duties of the Corps of the Royal Engineers*, vol. VIII. London 1844.

Ali Bey el-Abassi (1807). *Travels of Ali Bey ... between the Years 1803 and 1807.* London 1816 [1607].

Ali Bey el-Abassi (1807). *L'atlas des voyages d'Ali Bey ...* Paris 1814 [1607].

Allen, W. (1853). *The Dead Sea, a New Route to India ...* London 1855. 2 vols. [2306].

Armstrong, G. *Names and Places in the Old and New Testaments and their Modern Identification.* London 1888.

Armstrong, G. *The Raised Map of Palestine on the Scale of 3/8 Inch to One Mile.* London 1893.

Arundale, F. (1833). *Illustrations of Jerusalem and Mount Sinai ...* London 1837 [1781].

APES, (1871-7). *American Palestine Exploration Society Statements* I-IV. New York 1871-1877.

Assheton, J.T. (1820). *An Historical Map of Palestine or the Holy Land.* London 1820 [340-M].

Baedeker, K. *Palestine and Syria. Handbook for Travellers* (First Edition). London 1876.

Bannister, J.F. (1844). *Survey of the Holy Land, its Geography, History and Destiny* ... London 1844 [2040].

Barclay, J.T. (1855-7). *Jerusalem and Environs. From Actual and Minute Survey* ... Philadelphia 1856 [2447].

Barclay, J.T. (1855-7). *The City of the Great King, or Jerusalem, as it was, as it is, and as it is to be.* Philadelphia 1858 [2447].

Barclay, Sara J. (1855-7). *Hadji in Syria or Three Years in Jerusalem.* Philadelphia 1858 [2448].

Bartlett, S.C. (1873-4). *From Egypt to Palestine (a Journey Made in the Winter of 1873-4) through Sinai, the Wilderness, and the South Country* ... New York 1879 [3283].

Bartlett, W.H. (1842; 1853). *Walks in and about the City of Jerusalem* ... London 1844 [1970].

Bartlett, W.H. (1842; 1853). *Jerusalem Revisited* ... London 1855 [1970].

Basili, K. (1839-53). *Syrien u. Palästina unter der türkischen Regierung* ... Odessa 1862. 2 vols. [1918].

Beamont, W.T. (1854). *A Diary of a Journey to the East in the Autumn of 1854.* London 1856 [2357].

Bedford, F. (1864). *The Holy Land, Egypt, Constantinople, Athens, etc* ... London 1864 [2807].

Benjamin, I.J. (1846-51). *Eight Years in Asia and Africa from 1846 to 1855.* London 1865 [2130].

Berghaus, H. *Geographisches Memoir zur erklärung und erläuterung der Karte von Syrien.* Gotha 1835.

Bernatz, J.M. (1837). *Bilder aus dem heil. Lande* ... *Mit erläuterndem Texte von G.H. Schubert.* Stuttgart 1839 [1845].

Bertou, C.J. de (1838). "Voyage de l'extremité sud de la Mer Morte à la pointe nord du golfe Elanitique". *Bull. de la Soc. de Géogr.* 1838, X, 18-32; cf 84-100. [1872].

Bertrand, (1798-9). *Guerre d'Orient* ... *Campagne d'Egypte et de Syrie 1798-9* ... Paris 1847. 2 vols. [1557].

Beth-Hillel, D. (1832). *Travels from Jerusalem through Arabia, Koordistan, Persia and India.* Madras 1832 [1765].

Bonar, A.E. and R.M. M'Cheyne (1839). *Narrative of Mission of Inquiry to the Jews from the Church of Scotland in 1839.* Edinburgh 1846.

236

Bonar, A.R. (1844). *The Holy Land: Being Sketches of the Jews and of the Land of Palestine.* London 1844 [2041].

Bost, J.A. (1875). *Souvenirs d'Orient. Damas. Jérusalem* ... Paris 1875 [3322].

Bovet, F. (1858). *Egypt, Palestine etc...* London 1858 [2543].

Bremer, F. (1859). *Travels in the Holy Land.* London 1861. 2 vols. [2592].

Buchanan, R. (1857). *Notes of a Clerical Furlough Spent Chiefly in the Holy Land.* London 1859 [2505].

Buckingham, J.S. (1816). *Travels in Palestine through the Countries of Bashan and Gilead, East of the River Jordan.* London 1821. 2 vols. [1650].

Buckingham, J.S. (1816). *Travels among the Arab Tribes ... Including a Journey from Nazareth to the Mountains beyond the Dead Sea ...* London 1825 [1650].

Burckhardt, J.L. (1810-1812). *Travels in Syria and the Holy Land.* London 1822 [1627].

Burton, Isabel. *The Inner Life of Syria, Palestine, and the Holy Land.* London 1875. 2 vols.

Burton, R.F. (1872). *Unexplored Syria.* London 1872. 2 vols. [3199].


Callier, C. (1832). "Voyages en Asie Mineure, en Syrie, en Palestine et en Arabie-Petrée". *Bull. de la Soc. de Géogr.* 1835, III, 5-22, 239-262. [1763].

Carne, J. (1821). *Letters from the East.* London 1826. 2 vols. [1690].

Carne, J. (1821). *Recollections of Travels in the East Forming a Continuation of the Letters from the East.* London 1830 [1690].

Carne, J. (1821). *Syria, the Holy Land, Asia Minor, etc.* London 1835. 3 vols. [1690].

Castlereagh, L.V. (1845). *Narrative of his Journey to Damascus... Palestine and Syria.* London 1847. 2 vols. [2098].

Chasseaud, G.W. (1854). *The Druzes of the Lebanon, their Manners, Customs and History.* London 1854 [2360].

Chateaubriand, F.A. (1806-7). *Travels in Greece, Palestine, Egypt and Barbary during the Years 1806 and 1807.* London 1811 [1612].

Churchill, C.H. (1842-1852). *The Druzes and the Maronites under the Turkish Rule from 1840 to 1860.* London 1862 [2001].

Clarke, E.D. (1801). *Travels in Various Countries of Europe, Asia, and Africa.* Cambridge 1810-1823. 6 vols. Holy Land, Ch. III-IX [1600].

Clemens, S.L. (1867). *The Innocents Abroad: or the New Pilgrim's*

*Progress, Excursion to Europe and the Holy Land (by Mark Twain)*. Hartford 1870.

Clermont-Ganneau, Ch. *Recueil d'archéologie orientale*. 6 vols. 1881-1905. London 1899 [2970].

Conder, C.R. (1872-7). *Tent Work in Palestine*. London 1878. 2 vols. [3242].

Conder, C.R. and Kitchener, H.H. (1872-7). *Memoirs of the Survey Western Palestine*. London 1881-3. 3 vols. [3242].

Conder, C.R. (1872-7). *Map of the Palestine Exploration Fund during the Years 1872-1877*. London 1880 [3242].

Conder, C.R. (1872-7). *Palestine*. London 1889 [3242].

Conder, J. (1830). *The Modern Traveller*. London 1831 [1756].

Cooley, J.E. (1839). *The American in Egypt ... with Rambles through ... the Holy Land*. New York 1839 [1897].

Cook, T. *Tourist's Handbook for Palestine and Syria*. London 1891.

Cooper, W. *A Selection of Views in Egypt, Palestine, Rhodes ...* London 1822 [1696].

Curzon, R. (1834). *Visits to the Monasteries in the Levant*. London 1844 [1800].

Damer (Dawson), G.L. (1838). *Diary of a Tour in Greece, Turkey, Egypt and the Holy-Land*. London 1841-2. 2 vols. [1892].

Dixon, W.H. (1864). *The Holy Land, etc*. London 1864. 2 vols. [2851].

Döbel, E.C. (1834). *Wanderungen durch einen Theil von Europa, Asien u. Afrika ...* Gotha 1837-40. 2 vols. [1801].

Drake, C.F.T. (1871). *Unexplored Syria*. London 1872. 2 vols. [3167].

Dumas, A. et A. Dauzats (1839). *Quinze jours au Sinai*. Paris 1839. 2 vols. [1898].

Dupuis, L.H. (1852-3). *The Holy Places*. London 1856. 2 vols. [2305].

Egerton, Lady F. (1840). *Journal of a Tour in the Holy Land in 1840*. London 1841 [1921].

Elliot, C.B. (1836). *Travels in the Three Great Empires of Austria, Russia, and Turkey*. London 1838 [1829].

Fergusson, J. (1847). *An Essay on the Ancient Topography of Jerusalem*. London 1847 [2138].

Fergusson, J. (1847). *The Holy Sepulchre and the Temple at Jerusalem*. London 1865 [2138].

Fergusson, J. (1847). *The Temples of the Jews and other Buildings in the Haram Area at Jerusalem*. London 1878 [2138].

238

Finn, J. (1846-1863). *Byways in Palestine.* London 1868 [2987].

Finn, J. (1846-1863). *Stirring Times* ... London 1878. 2 vols. [2987].

Finn, E. Ann Mrs. (1846-1863). *Home in the Holy Land* ... London 1866 [2897].

Finn, E. Ann Mrs. (1846-1863). *A Third Year in Jerusalem* ... London 1869 [2897].

Finn, E. Ann Mrs. (1846-1863). *Palestine Peasantry.* London 1923 [2897].

Finn, E. Ann Mrs. (1846-1863). *Reminiscences* ... London 1929 [2897].

Fisk, G.A. (1842). *A Memorial of ... Jerusalem and other Principal Localities* ... London 1847 [1975].

Fisk, P. (1823). *A Memoir of ... Pliny Fisk late Missionary to Palestine.* Edinburgh 1828 [1701].

Forbin, L.N.P.A. Comte de (1817-18). *Voyage dans le Levant en 1817-18* ... Paris 1819 [1660].

Fraas, O. (1866). See: [2900].

Frankl, L.A. (1856). *Nach Jerusalem.* Leipzig 1856-61. 3 vols. [2459].

Frith, Fr. (1862). *Egypt, Sinai and Palestine ... 4 vols. with 150 Photographs, Views and Descript.* London 1862 [2739].


Gadow, H. (1848). See: [2171].

Gage, W.L. (Editor). *The Comparative Geography of Palestine and the Sinaitic Peninsula, By Carl Ritter, Translated and Adapted* ... Edinburgh 1866. 4 vols. [2901].

Geikie, C. *The Holy Land and the Bible ... 400 Original Illustrations by H.A. Harper.* London 1877.

Géramb, M.J. (1829-32). *Pèlerinage à Jérusalem et au Mont Sinai en 1831, 1832 et 1833.* Tournay 1836. 3 vols. [1741].

Georgi, O. (1845). *Die heil. Stätten nach Originalzeichnungen nach der Natur.* Leipzig 1854 [2081].

Graham, P. *Topographical Dictionary of Palestine or the Holy Land.* London 1836 [1830].

Grimm, J.L. (1830). *Palästina* ... Berlin 1830 [M-367].

Grove, G. (1861-3). "Nabloos and the Samaritans" in *Vacation Tourists and Notes of Travel 1861-3.* London 1862-4 [2728].

Guérin, V. (1854, 1863). *Description de la Palestine, Tomes I, II, III, Judée, Samarie, Galilée.* Paris 1868-75. 7 vols. [2369].


Harper, H.A. *The Bible and Modern Discoveries.* London 1889.

Harper, H.A. *Walks in Palestine* ... London 1894.

Harper, H.A. *An Artist's Walks in Bible Lands.* London.

Henniker, F. (1820-1). *Notes during a Visit to Egypt ... Mount Sinai and Jerusalem.* London 1823 [1687].

Herbert, Lady M.E. (1869). *Cradle Lands: Egypt, Syria, Palestine ...* New York 1869 [3046].

Herschell, R.H. (1843). *A Visit to my Father-land ... and Palestine in 1843.* London 1845 [2014].

Hogg, E. (1832-3). *Visit to Alexandria ... and Jerusalem during the Successful Campaign of Ibrahim Pascha.* London 1835. 2 vols. [1776].

Holthaus, D. (1842-45). *Wanderings of a Journeyman Tailor through Europe and the East during 1824 to 1840.* London 1841 [1708].

Horne, T.H. (1836). *Landscape Illustrations of the Bible ...* London 1836. 2 vols. [1832].

Hull, E. (1881-1882). *Mount Seir, Sinai and Western Palestine.* London 1885.

Hull, E. (1881-1882). *The Geology of Palestine and Arabia Petraea.* London 1886.

Hull, E. (1881-1882). *Reminiscences of a Strenuous Life.* London 1910.

Hunter, W.P. (1841). *Narrative of the Late Expedition to Syria under the Command of Admiral Sir Robert Stopford.* London 1841. 2 vols. [1952].

Isaacs, A.A. (1856-7). *The Dead Sea ... during a Journey to Palestine in 1856-7.* London 1857 [2496].

Isaacs, A.A. (1856-7). *A Pictorial Tour in the Holy-Land.* London 1862. [2496].

Irby, C.L. and Mangles, J. (1817-18). *Travels through ... Palestine ... in 1817-18.* London 1823. 2 vols. [1661].

Jacotin, M. (1799). *Carte topographique de l'Egypte et de plusieurs parties des pays limitrophes levée pendant l'expédition de l'armée française.* Paris 1810 [323-M].

Joliffe, T.R. (1817). *Letters from Palestine ... Galilee ... Judaea ...* London 1819 [1657].

Jones, G. (1836). *Excursions to Cairo, Jerusalem ... from the U.S. Ship Delaware ...* New York 1836 [1833].

Jowett, W. (1815-20). *Christian Researches in the Mediterranean from 1815-20.* London 1822 [1649].

Kamienietz, Menachem Mendel. *"Korot Haitim".* Vilna 1840.

Keith, A. (1844). *Land of Israel According to the Covenant with Abraham, Isaac and Jacob.* London 1844 [2058].

240

Kelly, W.K. (1844). *Syria and the Holy-Land.* London 1844 [2059].

Kent, S.H. (1874). *Gath to the Cedars. Travels in the Holy-Land and Palmyra.* London 1874 [3298].

Kerschbaumer, A. (1863). *Pilgerbriefe aus dem heil. Lande.* Wien 1863 [2780].

Kiepert, H. See: [M-431].

Kinglake, A.W. (1835). *"Eothen" or Traces of Travel.* New York 1845 [1817].

Kinnear, J.G. (1839). *Cairo, Petra and Damascus in 1839 ...* London 1841 [1901].

Kitchener, H.H. (1875). *Book of Photographs of Biblical Sites.* 1876 [3332].

Kitchener, H.H. (1875). Several Papers in the PEF. QSt. 1875, 1877, 1878, 1884 [3332].

Kitto, J. *The Physical Geography and Natural History of the Holy Land.* London 1841. 2 vols. [1953].

Kitto, J. *The Pictorial History of Palestine and the Holy Land.* London 1844. 2 vols. [1953].

Kitto, J. *Scripture Lands ... in a Series of Historical, Geographical and Topographical Sketches.* London 1850 [1953].

Klein, F.A. (1863). See: [2781].

Krafft, W. (1845). *Die Topographie Jerusalems.* Bonn 1846 [2082].


Laborde de, L.E. (1828). *Journey through Arabia Petraea to Mount Sinai ...* London 1836 [1731].

Lamartine, A. (1832-3). *Souvenirs, impressions, et paysages pendant un voyage en Orient.* Paris 1835. 4 vols. [1777].

Lartet, L. (1864). *Essai sur la géologie de la Palestine etc.* Paris 1870 [2822].

Legh, T. (1817-18). "A Journey from Moscow ... With a Continuation of the Route to Jerusalem". In *MacMichael*, W. London 1819 [1662].

Letronne, A.J. (1839). See: [1904].

Lewin, T. (1862). *The Siege of Jerusalem by Titus ...* London 1863 [2744].

Liebetrut, F. (1851). *Reise nach d. Morgenlande ... Jerusalem u. d. heil. Lande.* Hamburg 1854. 2 vols. [2254].

Liévin de Hamme. *Guide indicateur des sanctuaires et lieux historiques de la Terre Sainte.* (First Edition) Jerusalem 1869.

Light, H. (1814). *Travels in Egypt, Nubia, Holy Land, Mount Libanon and Cyprus.* London 1818 [1641].

Lindsay, A.W.C. (1837). *Letters on Egypt, Edom and the Holy Land.* London 1838. 2 vols. [1853].

Lortet, P. (1875-80). *La Syrie d'aujourd'hui. Voyages dans la Phénicie, le Liban et la Judée.* Paris 1884 [3377].

Löwinsohn, S. (1817). *Mehkere Eretz.* Wien 1819 [1659].

Luynes, A., Duc de, (1864). *Voyage d'exploration à la Mer Morte ...* Paris 1871-6. 3 vols. [2824].

Lynch, W.F. (1848). *Narrative of the United States Expedition to the River Jordan and the Dead Sea.* Philadelphia 1849. [2175].

Lynch, W.F. (1848). *Official Report ...* Baltimore 1852 [2175].

MacGregor, J. (1869). *Rob Roy on the Jordan ...* London 1870 [3053].

MacLeod, N. (1866). *Half Hours in the Holy Land. Travels in Egypt, Palestine, Syria ...* London 1884 [2907].

Mackworth, D. (1821-2). *Diary of a Tour through Southern India, Egypt and Palestine in the Years 1821-2.* London 1823 [1693].

Macmillan. *Guide to Palestine and Egypt.* London 1901.

Madden, R.R. (1824-7). *Travels in Turkey, Egypt, Nubia and Palestine in the Years 1824-7.* London 1829. 2 vols. [1707].

Madox, J. (1821-6). *Excursion in the Holy-Land ...* London 1834. 2 vols. [1694].

Manning, S. (1874). *Those Holy Fields. Palestine Illustrated by Pen and Pencil.* London 1874 [3300].

Mansell, A.L. (1862). *Coast Survey of Palestine, 1863* [2745; M-604].

Margoliouth, M. (1850). *A Pilgrimage to the Land of my Fathers ...* London 1850. 2 vols. [2229].

Mayer, J.H. (1813). *Reise nach Konstantinopel, Aegypten, Jerusalem ...* St. Gallen 1820 [1633].

Mayer, L. (1801-10). *Coloured Views from Original Drawings ... Vol. 3, Palestine, 24 Plates.* London 1804 [1603].

Merrill, S. (1874). *Galilee in the Time of Christ.* Boston 1881 [3318].

Merrill, S. (1874). *East of the Jordan; a Record of Travel and Observation in the Country of Moab, Gilead and Bashan During the Years 1875-7.* New York 1883 [3318].

Merrill, S. (1874). *Ancient Jerusalem.* New York 1908 [3318].

Millard, D.(1842). *A Journal of Travels in ... and the Holy Land.* Rochester 1843 [1981].

Molyneux (1847). See: [2150].

Monro, V. (1833). *Summer Rambles in Syria with a Tatar Trip from Aleppo to Stamboul.* London 1835. 2 vols. [1786].

242

Montefiore, M. & J. (1827-82). *Notes of a Visit to Egypt and Palestine.* London 1844 [1730].

Montefiore, M. & J. (1827-82). *Diaries*, edited by Dr. L. Loewe. Chicago 1890 [1730].

Moore, G.H. (1837). See: [1854].

Mott, Mrs. M. (1863). *Stones of Palestine* ... London 1865 [2801].

Munk, S. (1841). *Palestine. Description géographique, historique et archéologique.* Paris 1841 [1955].

Neale, F.A. (1846). *Eight Years in Syria, Palestine and Asia Minor from 1842 to 1850.* London 1851-2 [2114].

Neil, J. *Palestine Repeopled, a Sign of the Times.* London 1877 [3458].

Neil, J. *Palestine Explored with a View to its Present* ... London 1881 [3458].

Neil, J. *Pictured Palestine* ... London 1891 [3458].

Norow, A.S. (1835, 1861-2). *Reise nach d. heil. Lande im Jahre 1835.* St. Petersburg 1838. 2 vols. [1819].

Norow, A.S. (1835, 1861-2). *Jerusalem u. Sinai.* St. Petersburg 1878 [1819].

Olin, S. (1840). *Travels in Egypt ... and the Holy-Land.* New York 1843. 2 vols. [1930].

Oliphant, L. *The Land of Gilead.* London 1880.

Oliphant, L. *Haifa or Life in Modern Palestine.* London 1887.

Orelli, C. (1877). *Durch's heilige Land.* Basel 1878 [3460].

Osborn, H.S. (1855). *Palestine, Past and Present* ... London 1858 [2446].

PEF. (1865-9). *Palestine Exploration Fund Proceedings and Notes.* London 1865-9.

Palmer, E.H. (1870). *The Survey of Western Palestine. Arabic and English Name Lists.* London 1881.

Palmer, E.H. with Drake, T.C.F. (1870). *The Desert of the Exodus* ... London 1871. 2 vols. [3126].

Palmer, E.H. with Besant, W. (1870). *Jerusalem the City of Herod and Saladin.* London 1871 [3126].

Palmer, H.S. (1869). See: [3058].

Pardieu, C. (1849). *Excursion en Orient ... le Mont Sinai ... la Palestine.* Paris 1851 [2205].

Patterson, J.L. (1850). *Journal of a Tour in Egypt, Palestine, Syria and Greece.* London 1852 [2230].

Paxton, J.D. (1836-8). *Letters from Palestine* ... London 1839 [1843].

Pellé, C., and Galibert, L. (1843). *Voyage en Syrie et dans l'Asie Mineure* ... London & Paris 1843 [2034].

Pückler-Muskau, F.A. (1838). *Die Rückkehr Vom Verfasser d. Briefe eines Verstorbenen.* Berlin 1846-8. 3 vols. [1886].

Petermann, H. (1853). *Reisen im Orient.* Leipzig 1860-1 [2331].

Pfeiffer, I. (1842). *Visit to the Holy-Land* ... London 1844 [1983].

Pierotti, E. (1854-66; 1868). *Jerusalem Explored* ... London 1864. 2 vols. [2406].

Pierotti, E. (1854-66;1868). *Customs and Traditions* ... London 1864 [2406].

Porter, J.L. (1854-67). *The Giant Cities of Bashan and Syria, Holy Places.* London 1865 [2407].

Porter, J.L. (1854-67). *Jerusalem, Bethany and Bethlehem.* London 1887 [2407].

Prokesch, A. (1825). *Reise ins heilige Land Im Jahre 1829.* Wien 1831 [1736].


Ragusa, Herzog M.A. von (1834). *Voyage de M. le Maréchal Duc de Raguse en Hongrie* ... *en Syrie, en Palestine,* ... Paris 1837. 4 vols. [1802].

Raumer, K. von (1834). *Palästina.* Leipzig 1835 [1805].

Renan, E. (1860-1). See: [2688].

Rey, E.G. (1857-8). *Etude historique et topographique de la tribu de Juda.* Paris 1859 [2534].

Rey, E.G. (1857-8). *Voyage dans le Haouran et aux bords de la Mer Morte exécuté pendant les années 1857 et 1858.* Paris 1860 [2534].

Richardson, R. ( 1816-18). *Travels along the Mediterranean* ... London 1822. 2 vols. [1666].

Richter, O.F. (1815). *Wallfahrten im Morgenlande.* Berlin 1822 [1644].

Ritchie, W. (1856). *Azuba or the Forsaken Land* ... Edinburgh 1856 [2493].

Ritter, C. (1848). *Vergleichende Erdkunde der Sinai-Halbinsel von Palästina u. Syrien.* Berlin 1848-55. 14 vols. [2179].

Roberts, D. (1838-9). *The Holy Land from Drawings Made on the Spot.* London 1842-9. 3 vols. [1984].

Robinson, E. (1838; 1852). *Biblical Researches in Palestine* ... London, 1841. 2 vols. [1887].

Robinson, E. (1838; 1852). *Later Biblical Researches* ... London 1856 [1887].

244

Robinson, E. (1838; 1852). *Physical Geography of the Holy Land.* London 1865 [1887].

Robinson, G. (1830). *Travels in Palestine and Syria.* London 1837. 2 vols. [1746].

Rogers, Maria E. (1855-9). *Domestic Life in Palestine.* London 1862 [2450].

Rosenmüller, E.F.K. (1818). *Das alte u. neue Morgenland.* Leipzig 1818-20 [1667].

Russegger, J. (1835-41). *Reisen in Unter-Aegypten, auf d. Halbinsel des Sinai u. im gelobten Lande, 1847.* Stuttgart 1849 [1825].

Russell, M. (1830). *Palestine or the Holy Land from the Earliest Period to the Present Time.* Edinburg 1831 [1747].

Salzbacher, J. (1837). *Erinnerungen aus meiner Pilgerreise ... im Jahre 1837.* Wien 1839 [1856].

Salzmann, A. (1850-1, 1854, 1863). *Jérusalem étude et reproduction photographique des monuments de la Ville Sainte ...* Paris 1856 [2245].

Saulcy, F. de (1850-1, 1863). *Voyage autour de la Mer Morte ... exécuté de Décembre 1850 à Avril 1851 ...* Paris 1853. 2 vols. [2245].

Saulcy, F. de (1850-1, 1863). *Voyage en Terre Sainte.* Paris 1865. 2 vols. [2245].

Saulcy, F. de (1850-1, 1863). *Dictionnaire topographique ...* Paris 1877 [2245].

Saulcy F. de (1850-1, 1863). *Jérusalem.* Paris 1881 [2245].

Schick, C. *Beit el Makdas.* Jerusalem 1887 [2890].

Schick, C. "Improvement of Roads in Palestine." *Palestine Exploration Fund Quarterly Statement.* 1889, pp. 8-9 [2890].

Schick, C. "Preparations Made for the Visit of the German Emperor," *Palestine Exploration Fund Quarterly Statement.* 1899, pp. 116-117 [2890].

Scholz, J.M.A. (1821). *Reise in die Gegend zwischen ... Egypten, Palästina u. Syrien in d. Jahren 1820 u. 1821.* Leipzig 1822 [1691].

Schubert, G.H. (1837). *Reise in d. Morgenland in d. Jahren 1836 u. 1837.* Erlangen 1838-9. 3 vols. [1857].

Schultz, E.G. (1843-1855). *Jerusalem, eine Vorlesung.* Berlin 1845 [2039].

Schulz, E.W. (1851). *Reise in d. gelobte Land.* Mülheim 1852 [2260].

Schumacher, G. "Population Lists of the Liva of Akko," *PEF. QSt.* 1887. pp. 169-191.

Schumacher, G. *Across the Jordan ...* London 1886.

Schumacher, G. *The Jaulan*. London 1888.

Schumacher, G. *Abila, Pella and the Northern Ajlun*. London 1889.

Schwarz, J. (1832-3). *"Sefer Tebuôt Haaretz."* Jerusalem, (5605 =) 1845 [1778].

Schwarz, J. (1832-3). *A Descriptive Geography and Brief Historical Sketch of Palestine*. Translated by Isaac Lesser. Philadelphia 1850 [1778].

Seetzen, U.J. (1809). *A Brief Account of the Countries Adjoining the Lake of Tiberias, the Jordan and the Dead Sea* (Palestine Association of London). London 1810 [1615].

Seetzen, U.J. (1809). *Reisen Durch Syrien, Palästina, Phönicien ...* Berlin 1854-9. 4 vols [1615].

Sepp, J.N. (1845, 1874). *Jerusalem u.d. heil. Land ...* Hunter 1863. 2 vols. [2090].

Sieber, F.W. (1818). *Reise von Cairo nach Jerusalem ...* Leipzig 1823 [1669].

Skinner, T. (1834). *Adventures During a Journey ... and the Holy-Land*. London 1836 [1808].

Smith, G.A. (1880; 1899; 1901; 1904). *Historical Geography of the Holy Land*. Edinburgh 1894.

Smith, W. *Dictionary of the Bible Comprising its Antiquities, Biography, Geography and Natural History*. London 1860-3. 3 vols. [2689].

Spencer, J.A. (1849). *The East, Sketches of Travels in Egypt and the Holy Land*. London 1850 [2210].

Spilsbury, J.B. (1799-1800). *Picturesque Scenery in the Holy-Land and Syria Delineated During the Campaigns of 1799 and 1800*. London 1803 [1562].

Spyridon, S.N. "Annals of Palestine 1821-1841." *Journal of Palestine Oriental Society*. XVIII, 1-2, 1938, pp. 63-132.

Stanhope, Lady Hester. *Travels of Lady Hester Stanhope in Three Vols. Narrated by her Physician*. London 1845-1846.

Stanley, A.P. (1835, 1862). *Sinai and Palestine ...* London 1856 [2336].

Stanley, A.P. (1835, 1862). *Sermons Preached Before His Royal Highness, the Prince of Wales ...* London 1863 [2336].

Stebbing, H. (1847). *The Christian in Palestine, or Scenes of Sacred History. Illustrated from Sketches Taken on the Spot by W.H. Bartlett*. London 1847 [2156].

Stephens, J.L. (1836). *Incidents of Travel in Egypt, Arabia and the Holy Land*. New York 1837. 2 vols. [1838].

Stewart, R.W. (1854). *The Tent and the Khan, a Journey to Sinai and Palestine*. London 1857 [2389].

Strauss, F.A. (1845). *Sinai u. Golgotha, Reise in d. Morgenland.* Berlin 1847 [2093].

Taylor, Baron I.J.S. (1830). *La Syrie, l'Egypte, la Palestine et la Judée ...* Paris 1839. 3 vols. [1753].

Tennison, Lady L. (1846). *Sketches in the East by Lady Louisa Tennison.* London 1846.

Tischendorf, K. (1844, 1859). *Reise in d. Orient.* Leipzig 1846 [2067].

Tischendorf, K. (1844, 1859). *Aus dem heil. Lande.* Leipzig 1862 [2067].

Thomson, W.M. (1857 ...). *The Land and the Book ...* New York 1859. 2 vols. [1813].

Tobler, T. (1835-6; 1845-6; 1857; 1865). *Lustreise ins Morgenland.* Zurich, 1839. 2 vols [1824].

Tobler, T. (1835-6; 1845-6; 1857; 1865). "Reise von Jerusalem ... im Jahre 1846." *Ausland* 1846 [1824].

Tobler, T. (1835-6; 1845-6; 1857; 1865). *Denkblätter aus Jerusalem ...* Konstanz 1853 [1824].

Tobler, T. (1835-6; 1845-6; 1857; 1865). *Topographie von Jerusalem u. seinen Umgebungen.* Berlin 1853-4. 2 vols. [1824].

Tobler, T. (1835-6; 1845-6; 1857; 1865). *Planographie von Jerusalem ...* Gotha 1857 [1824].

Tobler, T. (1835-6; 1845-6; 1857; 1865). *Dritte Wanderung nach Palästina im Jahre 1857.* Gotha 1859 [1824].

Tobler, T. (1835-6; 1845-6; 1857; 1865). *Nazareth in Palästina nebst Anhang d. vierten Wanderung.* Berlin 1868 [1824].

Tobler, T. (1835-6; 1845-6; 1857; 1865). *Bibliographia Geographica Palaestinae.* Dresden 1875 [1824].

Tristram, H.B. (1863-4). *The Land of Israel, a Journal of Travels in Palestine.* London 1865 [2798].

Tristram, H.B. (1863-4). *Natural History of the Bible.* London 1867 [2798].

Tristram, H.B. (1863-4). *Bible Places or the Topography of the Holy Land ...* London 1872 [2798].

Tristram, H.B. (1863-4). *The Land of Moab ...* London 1873 [2798].

Tristram, H.B. (1863-4). *Pathways of Palestine ...* London 1881-2. 2 vols. [2798].

Tristram, H.B. (1863-4). *The Fauna and Flora of Palestine.* (The Survey of Western Palestine). London 1884 [2798].

Tristram, H.B. (1863-4). *Eastern Customs in the Bible Lands.* London 1894 [2798].

Turner, W. (1815). *Journal of a Tour in the Levant.* London 1820. 3 vols. [1646].

Van de Cotte, J. (1847). *Carte topographique de la Palestine* ... Bruxelles 1847 [M-506].

Van de Velde, C.W.M. (1851-2; 1862). *Narrative of a Journey through Syria and Palestine in 1851 and 1852.* London 1854. 2 vols. [2275].

Van de Velde, C.W.M. (1851-2; 1862). *Le pays d'Israel, Collection de cent vues prises d'après nature dans la Syrie et la Palestine.* Paris 1857 [2275].

Van de Velde, C.W.M. (1851-2; 1862). *Memoir to Accompany the Map of the Holy Land.* Gotha 1858 [2275].

Vignes, L. (1864). See: [2841].

Visino, J.N. (1837). *Meine Wanderung nach Palästina.* Passau 1840 [1860].

Vogüé de, M. (1853; 1871). *Fragments d'un journal de voyage en Orient.* Paris 1855 [2340].

Vogüé de, M. (1853; 1871). *Les églises de la Terre Sainte.* Paris 1860 [2340].

Vogüé de, M. (1853; 1871). *Le Temple de Jérusalem* ... Paris 1864-5 [2340].

Warburton, B.G. (1843). *The Crescent and the Cross* ... London 1844. 2 vols. [2028].

Warren, C. (1867). *Underground Jerusalem* ... London 1875 [2973].

Warren, C. (1867). *Survey of Western Palestine.* Jerusalem, London 1884 [2973].

Whitty, J.I. (1864). See: [2844].

Wigram, J.C. *The Geography of the Holy Land with References Which Serve as a Key to the Map of Palestine.* London 1837.

Wildenbruch, L. (1842-6). See: [2000].

Williams, G. (1843-4). *The Holy City* ... London 1849 (Second Edition) 2 vols. [2036].

Wilkie, D. (1841). *Original Sketches Comprising 26 Portraits and Sketches Taken in Turkey, Syria and Egypt.* London 1841-1843 [1959].

Wilson, C.W. (1864-1870). *The Ordnance Survey of Jerusalem.* Southampton 1866. 3 vols. [2891].

Wilson, C.W. with Palmer, H.S. (1864-1870). *Ordnance Survey of the Peninsula of Sinai.* Southampton 1869-72. 5 vols. [2891].

Wilson, C.W. with Warren, C. (1864-1870). *The Recovery of Jerusalem* ... London 1871 [2891].

Wilson, C.W. (1864-1870). (Editor). *Picturesque Palestine, Sinai and Egypt* ... London 1880. 4 vols. [2891].

Wilson, J. (1843). *The Lands of the Bible Visited and Described* ... London 1847. 2 vols. [2029].

Wilson, W.R. (1819). *Travels in the Holy Land* ... London 1822. 2 vols. [1676].

Wittman, W. (1800). *Travels in Turkey, Asia Minor and Across the Desert into Egypt, During the Years 1799, 1800 and 1801* ... London 1803 [1597].

Wolcott, S. (1846). See: [2127].

Wolff, M.S.A. (1822-3). *Missionary Journal and Memoir of the Rev. J. Wolff. Missionary to the Jews.* London 1824 [1699].

Woodcock, W.J. (1848). *Scripture Lands: Being a Visit to the Scenes of the Bible.* London 1849 [2183].

Woolley, C.L. and Lawrence, T.E. (1913-14). *The Wilderness of Zin.* Palestine Exploration Fund Annual, Third Volume, 1914-15.

Wortabet, G.M. (1856). *Bayroot, Syria and the Syrians or Turkey in the Dependencies.* London 1856. 2 vols. [2480].

Wylie, J.A. *The Modern Judaea Compared with Ancient Prophecy.* Glasgow 1841 [1960].

Wylie, J.A. *Ruins of Bible Lands, a Journey Over the Region of Fulfilled Prophecy.* Glasgow 1845 [1960].

Yanoski, J. et J. David (1848). *Syrie ancienne et moderne. Histoire et description.* Paris 1848 [2184].

Zimmermann, K. (1876). *Karten und Pläne zur Topographie des alten Jerusalems.* Basel 1876 [3417].

Zimpel, F. (1852; 1864). *Die Israeliten in Jerusalem.* Stuttgart 1852 [2298].

## B. SECONDARY SOURCES

The following list includes works about some of the most important explorers mentioned in this essay, as well as general books dealing with the history of the country in the 19th century.

**Amiran (Kallner), D.H.** "Jacotin's Map of Palestine" *Palestine Exploration Quarterly*, 76, 1944. pp. 157-163.

**Atlas of Israel**. Maps and Text I/4, I/5, VIII/1. Jerusalem 1970.

**Avitsur, S.** *Daily Life in Eretz Israel in the XIX Century*. Tel-Aviv 1972 (Hebrew).

**Ben-Arieh, Y.** "Pioneer Scientific Exploration in the Holy Land at the Beginning of the Nineteenth Century" *Terrae Incognitae, The Annals of the Society for History of Discoveries*, Vol. IV, 1972, pp. 95-100.

**Ben-Arieh, Y.** "Lynch's Expedition to the Dead Sea (1847/8)" *Prologue, The Journal of the National Archives*. Washington, D.C. 1973, Vol. 5, pp. 14-21.

**Ben-Arieh, Y.** "Fredrick Catherwood Map of Jerusalem — 1833" *The Quarterly Journal of the Library of Congress*. Washington D.C. 1974, pp. 150-160.

**Ben-Arieh, Y.** *A City Reflected in its Times, Jerusalem in the Nineteenth Century. The Old City*. Jerusalem 1977. (Hebrew).

**Ben-Zvi, I.** *Eretz-Israel under Ottoman Rule, Four Centuries of History*. Jerusalem 1962. (Hebrew).

**Besant, W.** *The Literary Remains of the late C.F.T. Drake*. London 1883.

**Besant, W.** *The Life and Achievements of E.H. Palmer*. London 1883.

**Besant, W.** *Twenty One Years' Work in the Holy Land of the Palestine Exploration Fund*. London 1895.

**Besant, W.** *Thirty Years' Work in the Holy Land of the Palestine Exploration Fund — A Record and a Summary*. London 1895.

**Bliss, F.G.** *The Development of Palestine Exploration*. London 1906.

**Blyth, E.** *When We Lived in Jerusalem*. London 1927.

**Bodenheimer, F.S.** *Canon Henry Baker Tristram (1822-1906). The Father of the Natural History of Palestine*. Tel-Aviv. 1957. (Hebrew).

**Boggis, R.J.E.** *Down the Jordan in a Canoe*. London 1939.

**Brugger, H.** *Die deutschen Siedlungen in Palästina*. Bern 1908.

**Courtenay, A.J.B.** *Joseph Barclay, Third Anglican Bishop of Jerusalem*. Missionary Biography 1883.

Corey, W.M. *From Rabbi to Bishop* (Michael Solomon Alexander). London (no date).

Daiches, S. *Lord Kitchener and his Work in Palestine.* London 1915.
De Hass, J. *History of Palestine: The Last Two Thousand Years.* London 1938.

Elat, E. "Claude Reignier Conder" *Eretz-Israel*, Vol. 7, Israel Exploration Society. Jerusalem 1964, pp. 158-170 (Hebrew).

Fedden, R. *English Travellers in the Near East,* London 1958.

Gat, B. *The Jewish Community in Eretz-Israel (1840-1881).* Jerusalem 1963 (Hebrew).
Gobat, Samuel, *Bishop in Jerusalem, His Life and Work.* London 1888.
Granovski, A. *Land Tenure in Eretz-Israel.* Tel-Aviv 1949 (Hebrew).
Grave, C.L. *The Life and Letters of Sir George Grove.* London 1903.

Hagen, V.W. von. *Frederich Catherwood, Architect.* New York 1950.
Hagen, V.W. von. *F. Catherwood, Architect-Explorer of Two Worlds.* Mass. 1968.
Hilprecht, H.V. *Explorations in Bible Lands During the 19th Century.* Edinburgh 1903, pp. 579-622.
Hoffman, C. *Occident und Orient.* Stuttgart 1926.
Hopkins, J.W.J. "Nineteenth-century maps of Palestine; dual purpose historical evidence" *Imago Mundi,* XXII, 1968, pp. 30-36.
Hopwood, D. *The Russian Presence in Syria and Palestine 1843-1914 Church and Politics in the Near East.* Oxford 1969.
Hurewitz, J.C. *Diplomacy in the Near and Middle East.* Princeton 1956. 2 vols.
Hyamson, A.M. *The British Consulate in Jerusalem in Relation to the Jews of Palestine.* London 1939-41. 2 vols.

Ish-Shalom, M. *Christian Travels in the Holy Land, Descriptions and Sources on the History of Jews in Palestine.* Tel Aviv 1965 (Hebrew).
Issawi, C. *The Economic History of the Middle East, 1800-1914.* Chicago 1966.

Karmon, Y. "An Analysis of Jacotin's Map of Palestine. *Israel Exploration Journal* 10, 1960, pp. 157-173; 241-254.

Lewis, B. *The Emergence of Modern Turkey*. London 1968.

Manuel, F.E. *The Realities of American-Palestine Relations*. Washington D.C. 1949.

Ma'oz, M. *Ottoman Reform in Syria and Palestine 1840-1861*. Oxford 1968.

Ma'oz, M. (Editor). *Studies on Palestine during the Ottoman Period*. Jerusalem 1975.

Masterman, E.W.G. "Three Early Explorers in the Dead Sea Valley: Costigan-Molyneux-Lynch" *Palestine Exploration Fund Quarterly Statements*, 44, 1911, pp. 12-27.

Oliphant, Margaret, W. *Memoir of the Life of Laurence Oliphant and of Alice Oliphant, his Wife*. London 1890, 2 vols.

Parkes, J.W. *History of Palestine from 135 A.D. to Modern Times*. Oxford 1949.

Röhricht, R. *Bibliotheca Geographica Palaestinae von 333 bis 1878*. Berlin 1890.

Rosen, F. *Oriental Memoirs of a German Diplomat*. London 1930.

Schattner, I. *The Map of Eretz-Israel and its History*. Jerusalem 1951 (Hebrew).

Schattner, I. "Ideas on the Physical Geography of Palestine in the early 19th century" *Eretz-Israel*, Vol. 2, Israel Exploration Society. Jerusalem 1953, pp. 41-49 (Hebrew).

Searight, Sara. *The British in the Middle East. A Social History of the British Overseas*. London 1969.

Sim, Katherine, *Desert Traveller, the Life of Jean Louis Burckhardt*. London 1964.

Temperley, H. *England and the Near East: The Crimea*. London 1936.

Tibawi, A.L. *British Interests in Palestine 1800-1901; A Study of Religious and Educational Enterprise*. Oxford 1961.

Tibawi, A.L. *American Interests in Syria 1800-1901: A Study of Educational Literary and Religious Work*. Oxford 1967.

Tibawi, A.L. *A Modern History of Syria including Lebanon and Palestine*. Edinburgh 1969.

252

Vilnay, Z. *The Holy Land in Old Prints and Maps*. 2nd edition. Jerusalem 1965.

Watson, C.M. *Fifty Years' Work in the Holy Land of Palestine Exploration Fund*. London 1915.
Watson, C.M. *The Life of Major-General Sir Charles Wilson R.E.* London 1915.
Williams, W. *The Life of General Sir Charles Warren*. Oxford 1941.

# INDEX OF PERSONS

256

# INDEX OF PLACES

# LIST OF ILLUSTRATIONS

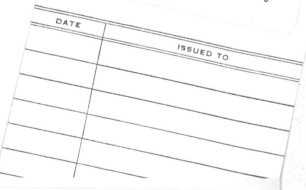